THE POTTER'S WHEEL

Barbaformosa

arts and crafts collection

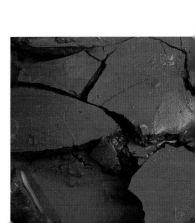

THE POTTER'S WHEEL

Original title of Spanish book:

EL TORNO

© Copyright Parramón Ediciones, S.A.,
1998–World Rights
Published by Parramón Ediciones, S.A.,
Barcelona Spain
Author: Barbaformosa
Illustrator: Louise Sylvester Toksvig
Photographer: Gabriel Serra
Graphic design: Josep Guasch
Translation: Mark Lodge
English text adapted and edited by
Eric A. Bye, M.A.

English edition © copyright 1999 by
Barron's Educational Series, Inc.

All inquiries should be addressed to:
Barron's Educational Series, Inc.
250 Wireless Boulevard
Hauppauge, New York 11788
http://www.barronseduc.com

International Standard Book No.
0-7641-5215-7

Library of Congress Catalog Card No.
99-72438

PRINTED IN SPAIN
9 8 7 6 5 4 3 2

INTRODUCTION, 6

Table of

MATERIALS AND TOOLS, 12

BASIC TECHNIQUES, 26

Contents

STEP-BY-STEP, 66

GLOSSARY, 158

BIBLIOGRAPHY AND ACKNOWLEDGMENTS, 160

Introduction

Will our traditional professions disappear with the passage of time? They may be lost if we fail to adapt them to modern life. I have worked for years with this in mind. Now I have brought together into one book the knowledge I acquired at the Massana School, and subsequently at the pottery workshops in 1968–69 in Esparreguera (Barcelona Province) in conjunction with the Sedó y Trujillo family.

Later I continued working in my studio, broadening and confirming what I had learned, until finally putting it into practice as a teacher at the Massana School, where I also spend part of my time doing research.

I acknowledge that mastering the wheel is complicated by the physical effort required, and many potters prefer to create the same pieces by other methods, which are sometimes slower, and at other times less creative. Just the same, the pleasure and magical feeling I get when working at the wheel more than compensate for the effort that's required even when you have mastered the skill. Creating a shape by pressing on a piece of clay, with the aid of the wheel, is a wonderful sensation.

In this book, I have tried to compile everything that I have learned over the years. I hope that it will help some people learn to throw, and that for others, it will help to dispel some of the doubts that arise through the long years of learning.

In this book, I sometimes refer to professional potters who throw all pieces on the wheel, always make the same traditional forms, and finish the pieces without turning them. This is the way some potters choose to work.

At other times, I refer to ceramists. These are professionals who use a variety of techniques for creating ceramic ware, including throwing. They take a more personal approach to ceramics and use the wheel for a variety of purposes.

Due to market demands produced by technological advances, these differences are becoming less important; as a result, we can simply refer in all cases to the professional who works with the wheel as a ceramist.

The layout of this book is based on that of the Arts and Crafts Collection, and is designed so you can easily locate whatever you need.

After a brief historical introduction, there is a chapter on materials and tools appropriate to the trade. This section treats the characteristics of different materials, and how to make and maintain some of the tools.

The next section explains some of the basic techniques; the most complicated ones are described in detail so that you can practice them individually. After this comes the how-to section, which presents the steps you need to follow in order to create certain shapes.

I was not able to include some basic pieces such as teapots and pitchers in this book. Given the breadth of this craft, I preferred to focus on the wheel as a tool for creating forms. All books that explain how to throw will include the pieces missing here. I believe that once you've gone through this volume, you'll be able to make those two pieces easily.

I have emphasized developing different ways of working on the wheel. I hope that everyone who works with the wheel will see it as a study of forms to create and discover, and not simply as a way of making utilitarian pieces, many of which are lacking in esthetic qualities.

The volumes, shapes, and objects should be evaluated in and of themselves, naked, without anything covering them to hide their defects. Many ceramists do not take this approach, evaluating the piece in the final phase, covered with glaze and in some cases, decorated without regard for the shape. For this reason, I intended to illustrate some chapters in black and white, with no additional elements to distract your attention from the shape.

Most ceramics manuals explain how to make pieces on the wheel, but then hardly touch on the next step in the process, which consists of turning the pieces.

Although not all pieces need to undergo this second phase, depending on your approach to the wheel, it is a fact that certain shapes simply cannot be made without turning.

The process of throwing is slow. In this book, the basics of throwing are presented precisely and thoroughly, with the greatest possible number of explanations. This will get you started properly and allow you to progress in the future without getting bogged down.

Hence the series of observations, suggestions, and analyses of finished pieces so that beginners will understand what they're doing, and at what level they're working.

At the same time, more experienced people will be able to see why they are not progressing in their mastery of the wheel and what the reasons are.

Those who simply want to play with different shapes and find easy ways to make particular pieces will find a variety of ways to make them, some easier than others.

With practice, you will come to know the material well, the level of moisture necessary to make different pieces, and how to handle them as they slowly dry throughout the process.

During the learning phase, you will come to know how the wheel can be used for each type of piece.

If you want to make a large quantity of pieces at a reasonable price, they should be turned only on the base or not at all, and merely thrown.

If, on the other hand, you want to produce pieces in small series or industrially, they should be thrown and turned to make them conform to the final pattern.

Another possible approach is to make artistic pieces, using the pieces that come off of the wheel as is, or deforming them, manipulating them, joining them, pressing them, etc.

In the final analysis, the wheel should do for us whatever we want it to, and serve as a tool for enjoyment and for creating diverse and magical forms.

To my mother

Barbaformosa was born in Barcelona in 1947. She studied ceramics at the Massana School in Barcelona and at Sunderland College of Art, England. She worked in the workshop of Jordi Aguadé and in the studio of Sedó de Esparreguera. Since 1981 she has been a member of the International Ceramics Academy of Geneva. She is an instructor at the Massana School and graduated in 1985 from the Barcelona Faculty of Fine Arts with a major in sculpture.

She has given many shows, and her work is on display in collections and museums such as the Ariana Museum, Geneva; Minar Sinan University, Istanbul; the Iris Collection, Porvoo, Finland; Umeleckprumyslové Museum, Prague; the Villa de Espluges Collection; the Alcora Ceramics Museum; Saga Prefectural Art Museum, Japan; and the Igal and Diane Silver Collection, California.

Barbaformosa has also published the book *Els secrets del Torn* (Secrets of the Potter's Wheel), published by Editorial Alta Fulla, Barcelona in 1991.

The author had her own studio in Barcelona from 1970 to 1985, then moved to the city of Girona, where she currently works.

History of the potter's wheel

The origin of the potter's wheel

There's not much written history concerning the potter's wheel, so its origins are uncertain and reported differently by scholars.

Will Durant and other archaeologists place the origin of the potter's wheel in the port of Susa (today Shushan), the most important of the cities of Elam. Around the year 4500 B.C., the Elamites conquered Sumer and introduced their technology there.

Mesopotamia's most important asset was its earth, which took on a unique consistency and hardness when dried. This contributed to the development of the wheel in that region. By studying the fingerprints on ancient pieces of pottery, researchers have concluded that the potter's wheel was in use in Mesopotamia as early as 3500 B.C., in Egypt as early as 2750 B.C., and in Sumeria from the year 2300 B.C. The Egyptians believed the god Khum had invented the wheel.

According to Jorge Fernández Chiti, the potter's wheel was invented in the Near East around 3500 B.C., and it spread out from two centers: the Egyptian Orient on the one hand, and China on the other. Nonetheless, some scholars believe that the Chinese wheel is indigenous to that area and has always existed, since the oldest Chinese porcelain pieces were made on a wheel.

Alex Brongniart contends that the potter's wheel was introduced to Europe by way of Greece, and even cites the name of its inventor: Tales or Thalos, an Athenian sculptor—nephew of the famous architect and sculptor Daedalus—who lived around the year 1,200 B.C. During the eighth century B.C., the potter's wheel reached Italy, and from there it spread throughout the Danube basin.

Pottery from North Africa and Spain is also thrown. It appears that the Arabs, a people renowned for their skill in ceramic arts, used the potter's wheel. Others maintain that the potter's wheel was first introduced into Spain during the sixth and seventh centuries B.C., becoming more widespread with the founding of Phoenician, Greek and Roman colonies, and that the Iberians quickly copied the techniques of the Phoenecian potters, adopting the potter's wheel in the process.

In the north and west of Europe ceramics known as *gales* or *celts* show clearly that they were made on a wheel. Surprisingly, large ceramic pieces, such as jars, pots, and amphoras, made in places where the potter's wheel was known, were not made on this tool, but rather with the banding wheel and with coils. The difference between these two procedures lies in the fact that with the potter's wheel the piece is spun in front of the potter, while with the banding wheel the potter moves around the piece.

Ancient pieces made by Scandinavian potters, although round in shape, were not made using a wheel.

Even though Germanic ceramics, which are difficult to distinguish from Welsh ceramics, including those made by the Gallo-Romans, are perfect pieces and essentially circular, they were not thrown on the potter's wheel; a banding wheel or some type of revolving plate was probably used.

Etruscan pottery, which includes some very perfect shapes, was likewise not made on a wheel. Some very thin gray or black Greek Etruscan ceramics appear to have been produced on a potter's wheel.

None of the ceramics from the pre-Colombian cultures of the two Americas and the Caribbean show signs of having been turned on a wheel, and that indicates that this instrument did not reach these cultures. Chronicles of that time relate the absence of the potter's wheel in producing ceramics and the natives' lack of interest in the instrument when they interacted with the Europeans. It is also known that wheeled vehicles were not in use, since they were not very practical in mountain regions and forest areas.

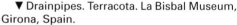
◄ Walls constructed with thrown pieces. Tokoname, Japan.

▼ Drainpipes. Terracota. La Bisbal Museum, Girona, Spain.

◀ Drainpipe elbows. Terra-cotta. La Bisbal Museum, Girona, Spain.

▶ **Bernard Leach.** *Porcelain bottle.*

The development of the potter's wheel

The potter's wheel is one of the earliest-known industrial instruments. It has evolved over the centuries from a slow, hand-operated wheel invented in the Neolithic Age, to the first recognizable potter's wheel around 4,500 B.C.

Its drive mechanism also developed over time, from operation by hand, foot, or an apprentice, to a wheel operated by electricity. The potter's wheel allowed potters to increase and improve their production, while at the same time satisfying the demands of a developing society.

Throughout history the potter's wheel has been used for a variety of purposes: for making utilitarian objects, such as containers for solids or liquids, food containers, and offering or funerary urns. Uses in the construction field include drainpipes and the building of walls in Tokoname, Japan using turned pieces.

Nowadays we can see magnificent thrown works that date from time immemorial. In the twentieth century, the creators of these works are unknown.

The twentieth century

During the twentieth century, some potters used the wheel to increase their production, and others to break away from traditional patterns. Trying to list all of them would be an immense undertaking and might prove uninteresting, since the potter's wheel was, and continues to be, one of the most important work tools of the ceramist. For that reason, only a few are presented here.

Bernard Leach

(1887–1979) Born in Hong Kong, he spent his childhood in Japan, and at the age of ten was sent to England to study at the Royal Art Academy. At the age of 21, he returned to Tokyo to acquaint himself with Oriental life and identify himself with Japanese culture, calling Japan the ceramist's paradise. He spent time in Beijing and Korea, where he studied Chinese pottery, and later returned to Japan.

Shoji Hamada

(1894–1978) This Japanese ceramist met Leach and they both went to England in 1920, where they founded a pottery workshop in St. Ives; this was the first pottery shop in that area.

Important changes began to take place in the English potters: they became artisans, rather than artists, adopting the Oriental technique of working, and Leach and Hamada rediscovered the slip decorating technique.

In 1923, Hamada returned to Japan, where later on he was declared a national treasure. He is regarded as the Japanese ceramist who did the most to foster Japanese ceramics in the eastern world.

Michael Cardew

(1901–1983) After graduating from Oxford, Cardew went to work in the pottery workshop in St. Ives. Later on he worked in Winchcombe, Wenford Bridge, and finally traveled to Africa, where he introduced the potter's wheel to that continent, first in the Gold Coast (Ghana) and later in Nigeria. He is also recognized as having introduced the potter's wheel to the Australian Aborigines. According to Hamada, Cardew possessed a great sensibility of form and attached the handles and spouts to his pieces with the same artistry as when he played the flute.

Bauhaus in Weimar

A design school located in Weimar between 1922 and 1925, it founded a ceramics school about 18 miles away in Dornburg de Sanle, in order to teach the old traditions in ceramics. Workshops, experienced assistants, and opportunities to obtain materials were greatly appreciated during the post-war period. In 1921, Gerhard Marcks was considered the master of form, influenced by his artistic and personal nature. He stimulated numerous students, such as Otto Lindig, among others, to explore forms based on the Spanish pitcher.

◀ **Hamada.** Bottle, *Hakémé*. Okinawa. Eleven inches high.

▶ **Otto Lindig.** Bauhaus. Weimar.

Lucie Rie

(1902–1995) An Austrian ceramist, attracted since childhood to Roman pottery, she worked in Vienna, at the same time as the Bauhaus school in Germany. Rie was inspired by architectonic forms of the Viennese secession. She emigrated to England prior to the Second World War.

Hans Coper

(1920–1981) A German sculptor, he worked with limited materials because he was interested in form. His pieces are combinations of two or more forms that are interrelated, frequently repeating those he found most pleasing. He was interested in contemporary architecture and worked for a time with Lucie Rie and with architects designing tabletop objects.

Pablo Picasso

(1881–1973) In 1950, the Spanish painter worked at the Madoura workshop, at Valluris in southeastern France. He used pieces turned on the potter's wheel as a form of expression. Some objects served as a basis for painting stories; he made them from assembled and decorated forms, and he manipulated others and turned them into new shapes.

Joan Miró

(1893–1983) The Spanish painter worked in conjunction with the ceramist Llorens Artigas; part of his work took the form of pots thrown on the wheel.

▲ **Lucie Rie.** *Bowl.* Porcelain. 3¹⁄₄ inches high by 11 inches in diameter.

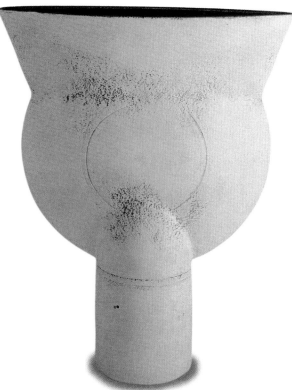

◄ **Hans Coper.** *Thistle Form.* Stoneware. 14¹⁄₄ inches high.

▼ **Miró-Artigas.** *Stoneware Pot.* 11 inches high. Paris Museum of Decorative Arts.

▼ **Pablo Picasso.** Model constructed from a thrown form. 5.1 inches × 9 inches. Dedicated to Mme. Ramié.

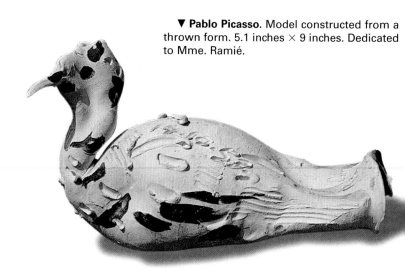

Antoni Cumella

(1913–1985) A Spanish ceramist, he did some of his work on a potter's wheel, creating a personal aesthetic and distinguishing himself with his pots that have wide, stable bases.

Michael Casson

(1925) English potter who has played a significant role in popularizing the potter's wheel. He has produced functional objects and has taught and lectured in the field of ceramics, both in England and in the United States. He has contributed to the resurgence of British ceramics. He was a founding member of the Craftsmen Potters Association of England. He produced a ceramics program for the BBC.

Daniel de Montmollin

(1925) French ceramist from the Taizè community, whose thrown pieces are inspired by objects from nature.

Petter Wolkos

(1924) During the first half of the 1950s his work consisted of altering classical circular forms in a quantity and on a scale never before seen. Potter's wheel exhibits revealed his confidence and improvisation in creating form. He took apart the shapes he made and then reconstructed them by joining the pieces.

Walter Keeller

(1942) English ceramist, skilled at throwing pieces that are at once utilitarian and sculptural objects. He studied with Casson and his work has contributed immensely to the techniques of the throwing.

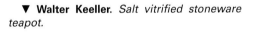

▲ **Petter Wolkos.** *Tsunami.* 15³/₄ × 12¹/₂ × 10¹/₂ inches. Stoneware. Am Adair Voulkos Collection.

◄ **Antoni Cumella.** 7¹/₂ × 10 inches.

▲ **Michael Casson.** *Stoneware jug.* Tenmoku.

▼ **Walter Keeller.** *Salt vitrified stoneware teapot.*

◄ **Daniel de Montmollin.** *White and red shino.*

Materials and tools

Three basic elements are required for throwing pottery: clay, a potter's wheel, and some tools.

There are many different types of clay to choose from according to its plasticity, roughness or smoothness, and color.

Some types are more suitable than others for creating certain forms, or for achieving a desired final product. Knowing the differences can help us make the right choice in all instances.

There is a wide variety of potter's wheels to choose from, some of which are easier to use than others, although with practice, you can get used to any wheel. The choice of machine is often governed by price and the nearest supplier.

Finally, there are the tools. This section is fairly long because all the tools are examined in depth—how to maintain them, and in certain cases, how to make them. Practice shows us that only four tools are used, and they are almost always the same ones, selected according to the work being done.

The choice of these elements, together with their appropriate maintenance and use, will help us to enjoy the art of throwing ceramics.

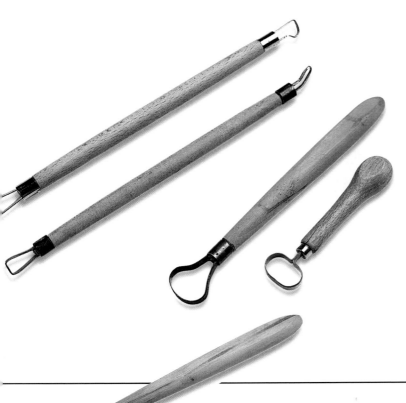

The clay

The basic material required for throwing is clay. It must be so plastic that the body can be pressed into a shape and maintain it even after you have stopped pressing.

Not all clays are suitable for throwing; for this reason ceramists have always tried to set up shop close to clay deposits, and ideally, to own or to lease a plot of land to ensure that they have material to produce ceramics over a long period of time. Most of the procedures used to extract earth and produce clay are based on practice and experience. This procedure is the cheapest, but not necessarily the most precise one, in terms of the consistency of the material used. If you want earth of the highest quality, you will have to have it analyzed chemically. Although this will increase the cost, you will be assured a constant quality.

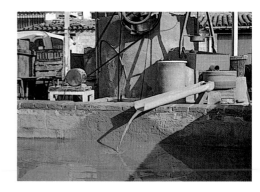

▲ **1.** Until recently, potters would dig up the earth with a pick and shovel and transport it to their workshop. Once there, it was spread out onto a threshing floor for a while, where it was ground and sieved, and placed in a machine where water was added for mixing.

▲ **2.** Once the earth was mixed with water, it was poured into reservoirs where the clay was left to settle and the water to evaporate.

◄ **3.** When the clay began to dry, and before it could crack, it was divided up into segments using stick with a metal tip like a knife blade. That way, once the clay was dry, it was already cut into predetermined shapes.

▲ **5.** When the clay had the right moisture content, the blocks were removed and stored in a warehouse for use throughout the year.

◄ **4.** The heaviest clay, containing the most sand, collected at the lowest point of the reservoir. It was used for other purposes such as manufacturing roofing tiles and bricks.

▼ **6.** Today, excavators are used to dig the earth. First, holes about eight to ten yards deep, depending on the terrain, are dug into the ground in the area to be worked. If the area is found to contain clay, excavation continues.

▼ **8.** The clay is dug up and piled in layers of between twenty and twenty-four inches deep. They are left to lie for seven to eight months, so that rain can penetrate into their interior.

▲ **7.** It is very rare to find clay that contains all the properties necessary to throw pottery on a wheel. Sometimes, it is necessary to search for different types of earth in different places and then mix them together. It is also possible to find all types of clay in a single area, arranged in layers called seams.

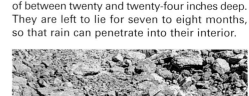

▲ 9. Huge piles are made with earth of the same color, and depending on how it's mined, they are left for quite a while; sometimes vegetation even begins to grow on top.

▲ 10. When the earth has settled as much as possible, sometimes for an entire generation, it is transported to the factory, where it is ground, sieved, and mixed with water until it becomes a paste. Filters are filled with liquid clay to remove excess water, and an hour or two later, depending on the type of filters used and the surrounding temperature, the clay is removed.

◄ 11. Next it is emptied into a pugmill to be mixed and homogenized.

Different types

Common clays

Most natural clays fall within this category. They contain iron and other mineral impurities that tend to be red (A), brown (B), greenish or gray, and least common of all, white. In certain cases they are worked with manganese oxide additives, as in the case of (C).

These clays are fired at between 1750° and 2000° F. They are all porous, so they are not suitable for containing liquids, which they will absorb. However, this characteristic is sometimes put to use in making vessels to hold water. As the water seeps through the clay, it keeps cool; this is a characteristic of certain pitchers.

Once fired, the clay may vary in color, including pink, beige, brown, tan, red, or black, depending on the clay and the firing conditions.

We recommend learning with one of these clays, since they are the easiest to work with and reasonably priced.

▼ Common clays.

B

A

C

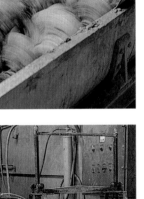

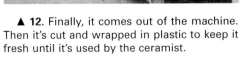

▲ 12. Finally, it comes out of the machine. Then it's cut and wrapped in plastic to keep it fresh until it's used by the ceramist.

China

Known as *faïence*, after the pottery city of Faenza in northern Italy, china is a porous clay. That porosity can range from between six and twenty percent, depending on the composition of the paste. It is not fired at a vitrification temperature, and that's why it's porous. It's not recommended for containing liquids, since a vessel will slowly absorb water and darken in color at the same time.

▲ China

It is fired at between 1870° and 2100°F. The higher the temperature, the more compact and denser it is, reducing the degree of porosity, but never actually reaching the same degree of vitrification that stoneware does.

China is a white clay, although glazed and decorated pieces of red ware are also called china, a technique introduced by the Arabs in the south of Spain.

It's normally quite difficult to throw, although it's not possible to generalize, since there are several varieties.

China can be used to make decorative objects. When this type of clay is fired at low temperature, it can be decorated with a broader range of colors, since some of these disappear at higher temperatures. Reds, oranges, and yellows are the most difficult colors. Although the clay can be glazed to protect its porosity—or in other words, a surface layer of glass is applied—the contractions of the clay and the glaze are not normally the same, and the glaze tends to crack. It is easy to recognize a piece of china because it is thicker and lighter than porcelain, and it is not as white.

Stoneware

This type of clay is fired at a high temperature of between 2200° and 2370°F. It is a dense, compact, and vitreous clay. Stoneware has a low degree of porosity, between one and three percent, meaning it is impermeable to water; for that reason it's ideal for containing liquids.

Stoneware may be light and pinkish in color (A) or cream-colored (B), among others. There are also dark types, such as this brown example (C), which is a natural stoneware; that is, the earth from a specific place has all the essential characteristics required for throwing just as it's found in nature.

Stoneware is not as white as porcelain. It is more difficult to throw than other clays, but less so than certain types of china. Pieces thrown on the potter's wheel cannot be made as thin as those made with common clays. If you want to use it for throwing very thin pieces, because you don't want to turn them,

A

▲▼ Stoneware

B

C

▲ Porcelain

▼ Refractory Clay

D

E

a little grog must be added to the clay. Grog is a finely ground fired clay that is mixed with other clays in various proportions to prevent warping, and in the case of throwing, to make the clay easier to work. If these pieces are turned, the grog comes to the surface and leaves grooves in it.

Porcelain

Porcelain is a clay composed of feldspar and kaolin. It is fired between 2200° and 2550°F according to the type of paste, until it reaches its point of vitrification. Once fired, it should possess between 0.5 and one percent absorption.

It is ideal for containing liquids and is highly valued for all types of uses: crockery, decorative objects, and chemical, industrial, and technological uses.

Porcelain is white, the feature that most distinguishes it from stoneware. It is appreciated for its solidity, its whiteness, the sound it makes when tapped, and its translucence.

This is a difficult and compact clay to throw, so it's best used once you have mastered the potter's wheel. The harder a clay is to work, the better it is for making a thin vessel. Thrown porcelain pieces are turned to achieve the fine body characteristic of this type of material.

Refractory Clay

This clay is a mixture of kaolin, aluminum oxide, and grog. The result is a fairly porous material that begins to vitrify at 2370°F, and can melt at 2900°F or more, depending on the type. Refractory clay can contain up to 30 percent grog, and depending on the size of the granules, may produce one type or another of refractory clay, thus making it impossible to turn the pieces on the wheel, or sometimes to throw them at all.

There is a wide range of colors of refractory clay, depending on the clay being used. In this reddish-colored type (D), the size of the grog can barely be detected, while in (E), it is easy to see.

Refractory clay is not a body that's used for throwing, unless it contains very fine grog.

If, despite everything, you want to throw this type of clay, we recommend using rubber gloves to protect your hands, unless the grog is so fine you can't feel it.

The potter's wheel

There are many kinds of potter's wheels and different ways to position yourself in front of them for throwing. Work methods are usually passed down by tradition. Foot-powered wheels were traditional among potters for many years, until the advent of electricity. Some craftsmen added motors to their old machines. This allowed them to be operated by foot or electrically. Others exchanged their foot wheels for electrically-operated wheels, retaining the large work surfaces around them. The tables allowed potters to place the objects being made to one side while continuing to work.

Because of trips to Japan by some professional ceramists, Japanese wheels were imported; their small size made them popular among some ceramists. The work procedure changed, and pieces were now thrown from in front. For this reason, nowadays it's easy to choose the position you prefer for throwing ceramics on the wheel.

▶ With the discovery of electricity, the potter added a motor to the foot wheel to make it easier to operate.

▶ Studies carried out on the human body prove that effort exerted when the body is positioned sideways doubles the strain on the back. For this reason, the potter's wheel was modified so that it could be used from the front. At the same time, a backrest was added to the seat so that the ceramist could take occasional breaks.

▼ A Japanese wheel. The worker sits directly in front of it. It has neither a seat nor a water container built in. It is equipped with handles to make it easier to carry.

◀ This type of potter's wheel is known as a foot wheel. It's the most traditional type, and was once the most commonly used. This one is located in La Bisbal and is a museum piece. You can see how the wood was worn down through use over the years. In order to operate it, the user must sit sideways to the wheel, due to the size of the lower wheel.

▲ Other potters preferred to change their machine and design a new one. Despite this, they continued to sit in the same position as when operating the foot wheel. Since the wheel head turns in a counterclockwise direction, the ceramist has to work on the right side.

▲ This potter's wheel was inspired by the Japanese wheel. The device is operated while sitting in front of it. The water container is located under the wheel head, and there is no built-in seat.

◀ A Japanese wheel. It is used while seated in front of the device. It has a built-in seat but no basin.

▲ An English potter's wheel. This wheel allows the ceramist to work seated or standing. When the worker is seated, the handle is operated manually, but it also has a pedal. If the worker stands, one leg must be inserted into the yoke to control the speed.

▶ A Nepalese potter's wheel operated with a stick. (Musée de l'home, Paris, France)

◀ Another way of throwing, using a helper to operate the wheel.

▲ The traditional Japanese procedure entails working on very low potter's wheels whose wheel head spins in a clockwise direction. This means that the potter must work on the left-hand side of the wheel.

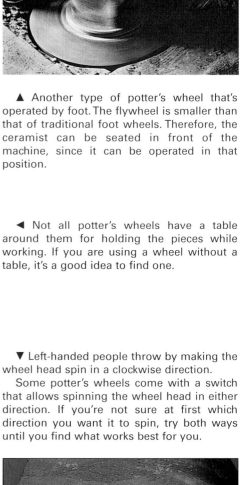
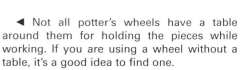

▲ Another type of potter's wheel that's operated by foot. The flywheel is smaller than that of traditional foot wheels. Therefore, the ceramist can be seated in front of the machine, since it can be operated in that position.

Other tools

The ceramist needs several tools to facilitate throwing. They are cheap, and assuming a modicum of skill, the ceramist can even make them from scrap materials.

◀ Not all potter's wheels have a table around them for holding the pieces while working. If you are using a wheel without a table, it's a good idea to find one.

▼ In certain pottery-manufacturing areas it's usual to work with a wooden shelf placed next to the wheel to hold the pieces being made.

▼ Left-handed people throw by making the wheel head spin in a clockwise direction.
Some potter's wheels come with a switch that allows spinning the wheel head in either direction. If you're not sure at first which direction you want it to spin, try both ways until you find what works best for you.

▼ In order to obtain maximum efficiency from the potter's wheel, a second wheel head can be added, of either the same size or larger. This is installed with an Allen wrench; other plates are secured with a screw.

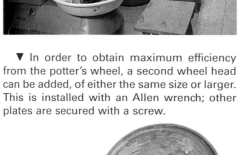

◀ A solid wood plank makes an ideal surface for wedging the clay. The wood doesn't need to be varnished, and it should be porous so the clay doesn't stick to the surface during the wedging process.

▶ You can also use a piece of chipboard or other compact type of conglomerate, but make sure that as the wood wears down, no pieces get mixed in with clay. That's a reason to avoid excess moisture.

▶ The ideal height of the wedging table should be 8 to 10 inches below the elbow. That way the energy for wedging comes from the arms and not from the back. Just the same, ceramists have always wedged on lower surfaces because it is less tiring.

▶ The shelves can be permanent or adjustable. They should be made according to the requirements of the pieces you intend to produce; you'll need to consider the weight the shelves will support, and you may need to reinforce them. Potters generally use adjustable shelves.

▲ It's a good idea to place a table against the wall so that you don't have to move around when wedging. If the table is located in the center of the room, it should be sturdy.

▼ Modern technology provides some sophisticated storage options.

◀ Any kind of sink is useful, but make sure that the clay doesn't get into the drain and plug it up.

Faucets should be easy to turn on and off with wet hands.

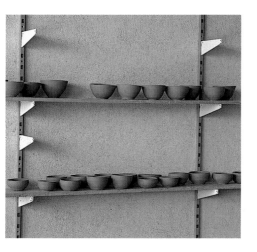

▶ Ideally, the clay should be kept in a damp place where it can be piled according to moisture content. If this isn't practicable, you can simply store the clay in plastic or some other type of container. Be sure that the containers aren't affected by moisture.

The tools

In order to master the potter's wheel, it is important to know how to use and maintain the tools, and which type of clay is most appropriate for each tool.

If the ceramist can also make or alter the tools for various needs, their use for every purpose will be that much clearer, and they will be perfectly adapted for their intended use.

The tools fall into two main categories: tools for throwing, and tools for turning. Among the latter, it's important to distinguish which ones are best for which type of clay. Tools should be used only for the specific purpose they're designed for; otherwise you may damage them.

There is a wide range of tools available on the market, and some of them are difficult to use. Therefore, in these pages we have chosen tools that are easiest for beginners to use.

General tools

You should keep a toolbox with the basic tools for modifying or making tools used for throwing.

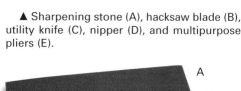

▲ Sharpening stone (A), hacksaw blade (B), utility knife (C), nipper (D), and multipurpose pliers (E).

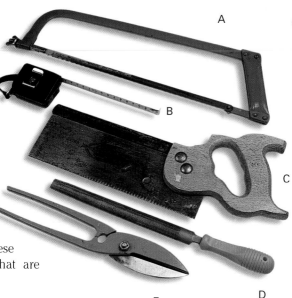

▲ Hacksaw (A), measuring tape (B), wood saw (one saw or the other will suffice) (C), file (D), and tin snips (E).

▲ 100- and 220-grit sandpaper (A), emery cloth (B), pencil (C), and hand drill (D).

Tools used for throwing

Here are some of the tools that are used for throwing pieces from soft clay on the potter's wheel.

Short, thin needle tool

This tool can be purchased in varying sizes. A thin needle is good. If it's thick, be sure there are no abrupt changes in thickness. In that case, you'll have to smooth them out with a sharpening stone.

The needle tool is used for cutting the mouth of the pieces. A needle an inch-and-a-half long is adequate for this task. Any type of handle can be used, since no pressure is needed while working. Don't leave this tool in water, or the metal ferrule will come loose if it's not firmly attached.

Long needle tool

This needle is thicker and stiffer than the previous one. The point must be sharp, and the needle must be even all the way to the end. If not, you'll have to modify it. The handle has to be thick to afford a good grip, since you'll need to use some force. The length of the needle should be about four inches in order to work properly. If it's much longer, it will be harder to control. This tool is used for modifying chucks.

▼ Needle tools are often sold poorly sharpened. The needle must gradually increase in diameter from the point to the handle. The first two drawings (B and C) show two needle tools that are made incorrectly and need to be fixed with a sharpening stone. To check if the needle is made correctly, hold the needle at one end between your thumb and index finger and run your fingers over it from one end to the other; if there are no bulges, as in illustration (A), the tool is perfect for working with.

If you can't find a suitable needle tool in your local store, you can easily make one yourself by grinding down a screwdriver on a grinding wheel. The ideal measurements are 5/32 of an inch in diameter and four inches in length.

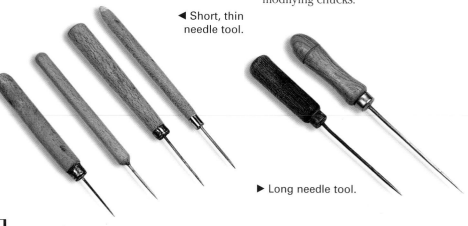

◄ Short, thin needle tool.

► Long needle tool.

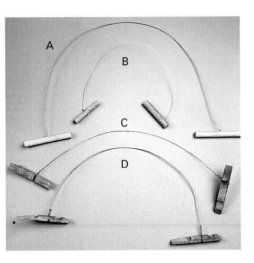

▲ Cutting Wire: Steel wire (A), nylon wire (B), thin steel wire (1/64" piano wire) (C), copper wire (D).

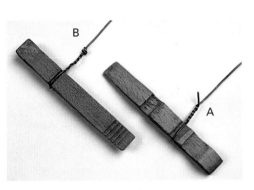

▲ You can make your own cutting wire from fourteen inches of 1/64 inch steel wire or .020 inch copper wire, or nylon line of the same thickness, and a clothespin. If you use metal wire, make sure that once the wire is twisted around the peg and itself (A), the end is tucked in toward the pin (B) so that it doesn't stick you when you're working.

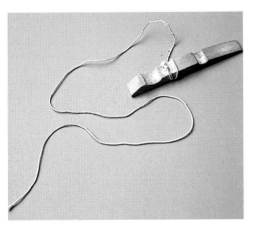

▲ Cutting wire for cutting lumps.
• Materials required: cotton cord (available in many places); one clothespin.
• Instructions: Cut a length of wire about 10 inches in length and tie one end to each half of the clothespin.

Cutting wire

The cutting wire is a foot long, with a piece of wood attached to each end. If you are working with big pieces, the wire will have to be longer, but if the pieces are normal in size, the longer the wire, the more difficult it is to use.

If metal cutting wires bend, they leave marks on the clay. The toughest and thinnest wire is piano wire. When used to cut the base of large pieces, it leaves less clay on the wheel, because of its thickness and toughness.

Nylon line is the most practical because it cuts easily.

Cutting wire for cutting lumps

You can't buy this tool in a store, so you'll have to make it yourself. All you need is a cotton thread or any tough material that doesn't revert to its original form when it's rolled up. This is different from steel wire and nylon line.

Cutting wire is used for cutting pieces made from a lump of clay while the wheel head is revolving.

The rib

This metal tool measures from one- to two-thirty-seconds of an inch in thickness. It should be made of a material that's not affected by moisture, such as copper or stainless steel. Ribs normally have right angles, but there are some variations. This tool should have a hole in the center about an inch in diameter. Manufacturers have reduced the size of the hole so that it serves only for hanging, so the tool is often held in a different way.

This is one of the few pleasant tools used in potters' workshops. For many ceramists, on the other hand, this tool has become little more than a rusty piece of tin that's lost some of its usefulness.

This tool is continually used for a wide variety of functions: for leveling and smoothing pieces, and for stretching the clay as it's worked.

Wooden caliper

Calipers can be made of wood or metal. If they are made of wood, it should not be a porous type, or they will absorb moisture. Curved compasses are used to measure the outside diameter of pieces. The straight variety is used to measure the height and the internal diameter.

Aluminum compass or caliper

The aluminum type does not rust and is easy to adjust.

Depending on its position, this caliper is used to measure the inside and outside dimensions as well as the height. However, when you are throwing a flat base, this instrument is not the most useful for measuring the clay.

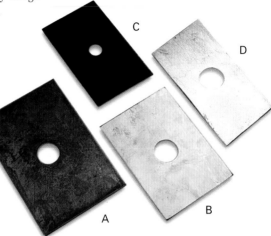

▲ Correct way of holding a rib when working.

▲ Copper ribs (A, B), an iron rib (C), and a stainless steel rib (D).

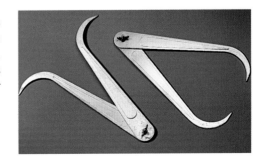

▲ A wooden caliper.

▼ An aluminum caliper.

Wooden tools

These tools must be thin and easy to handle, and the tip must come to a knife point. They are used for removing clay burrs from the bases of objects made on a plaster bat without scratching them. The wooden tools on the market don't work very well, so the tips have to be modified with sandpaper.

Cane smoothing tool

This tool is a 3½-inch strip of cane. You can't buy it in stores, but it's easy to make. Split the cane down the middle by wedging a knife into one end and using it as a lever.

Potters use this tool to smooth pieces and to narrow the necks of pieces.

Cane is the ideal tool for smoothing a piece on the wheel head. Once the piece is leather-hard, it is placed on a chuck; with the wheel turned on, the cane is moved from top to bottom, applying pressure to the piece to smooth it. If the piece is too dry, it can be moistened a little with a sponge, but not too much, or the surface may crack.

Sponges

It's best to use natural sponges with few holes. Dense synthetic sponges can also be used. They are used to finish pieces and remove excess water from the inside. In some cases you can use them to smooth the clay on the base if your fingertips haven't been trained to do it. In this manual sponges are not used to remove water, because from the beginning the emphasis is on controlling excess moisture, thereby avoiding many defects.

▲ Cane smoothing tool.

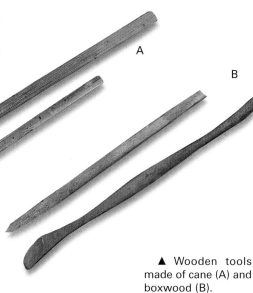

A

B

▲ Wooden tools made of cane (A) and boxwood (B).

▲ Sponges.

Turning tools

Turning tools are used to finish pieces while they dry. There are two types: ones that are not used for cutting, and ones that are. The former are used while the clay is still soft, and the latter when the clay is drier and hard.

The wire loop tool is part of the first group.

For tools of the second type to work properly, they must be well sharpened, unless the metal is thin and tough.

The wire loop tool

This tool gets its name from the loops at either end. It is not available in stores, but it is easy to make. You can find similar pieces in stores, but the metal is thicker; they don't work well, and once they break from applying too much force, the loops cannot be replaced.

This type of tool is used for removing excess clay while it's soft, as well as for eliminating lumps that appear during the turning process. For this tool to work correctly, the loop has to be securely fastened to the handle so it doesn't move in use.

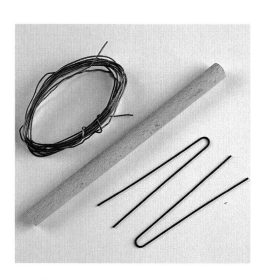

▲ Materials required:
2 large hairpins.
1 length of half-inch dowel.
2 half-inch lengths of copper wire about .020 inch thick.

The copper wire must wrap snugly around the stick; if it has been tempered or is not made entirely of copper, it will not tighten down properly and hold the clips.

◀ Wire loop tool.

▼ 1. Cut about a 5 inch section of dowel (A). Taper the ends a little with a file (B).

Draw a 1 inch line at one end of the dowel. Using a utility knife or a thin saw, cut a slot that matches the size of the copper wire on the line you have drawn. Drill a hole at the end of the groove about an inch from the tip. Repeat the operation for the other end of the dowel so that both slots are parallel (C).

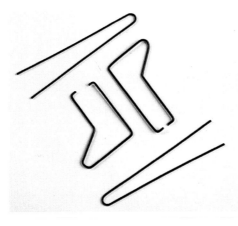

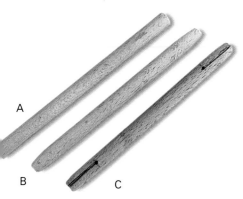

A

B   C

▶ 3. Fit the bent ends of the hairpins into the holes. Use the pliers to squeeze the pin into the groove firmly to anchor it.

Cut a length of copper wire about 31 inches long and wind it around the dowel. Put the end of the wire on one side of the pin, and hold the tool with one hand while you stretch the wire with the other. Keep winding until it is as taut as possible.

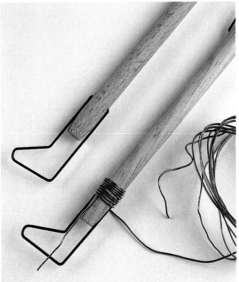

◄ 2. Open up the hairpin a little. Bend it from the center, $^3/_4$ inch on one side and $1^1/_4$ inch on the other. The best way to do this is to hold the clip with pliers and bend it with your hands. If you try to correct any mistakes, you'll score the metal, so you should use another clip.

Cut the legs so that they match, and then bend each one inward about $^5/_{64}$ inch from the end.

Repeat the operation with another clip, but this time bend it 1 inch at one end and $^3/_4$ inch at the other.

The main thing with these tools is that one is smaller than the other, and one has longer legs than the other.

▼ 4. Intertwine the two ends of the wire together where they meet (A).

Cut the wire off, leaving a little more than an inch, and tuck it into the end of the dowel so it doesn't stick you when you're using the tool. Repeat the procedure on the other end. If you have done it correctly, the hairpin will be securely fastened with a minimum gap of a $^1/_2$ inch between the two angles. Otherwise, you should start over (B).

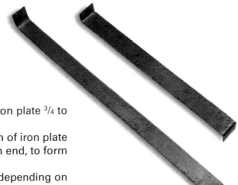

A

B

Angle tools

This is one of the traditional tools used in some pottery studios. It is not used very much because it digs into the clay easily. It is not available in stores.

If you want one of these you should have a blacksmith make one. It's made from a piece of metal an inch or two wide. The cutting part is the widest, measuring between $3^1/_2$ and $4^3/_4$ inches. The center measures from $2^3/_4$ to $3^1/_4$ inches; the total length, therefore, is between ten and twelve inches. The longest one measures twenty inches. This tool must be kept sharp. I usually don't recommend this tool because there is another one that does the same thing, causes fewer problems, and can be made by ceramists themselves: a flexible rib.

The flexible rib

This tool is easy to make and use. Since it is not sold in any store, you'll have to make it yourself.

◄ Angle tools.

▶ Flexible rib.
• Materials: A piece of polished iron plate $^3/_4$ to 1 inch wide and $^1/_{10}$ inch thick.
• Instructions: Cut a 12 inch length of iron plate and make a right-angle bend at each end, to form the shape of a Z.

You can have tools of two sizes, depending on the pieces you intend to make.

Small trimming tool

There are many tools of this type to choose from. If they are made of thick metal, they need to be sharpened. This is not necessary if the metal is thin, as long as the quality is good.

Trimming tools are used for turning the bases of small pieces and for working in areas that are difficult to reach. In order to keep them in good condition, they should be kept dry.

Round trimming tool

There are several types of round trimming tools available on the market. When you buy these tools, be sure they are sharp and that the handle is comfortable to the hand. Some handles are too big for many people's hands. This tool should not be allowed to get wet. It is used for working inside curved pieces.

Home-made trimming tool

This tool is used only by certain ceramists. It consists of an iron loop, the handle of which is covered with adhesive tape or copper wire; in the latter case the tool weighs more.

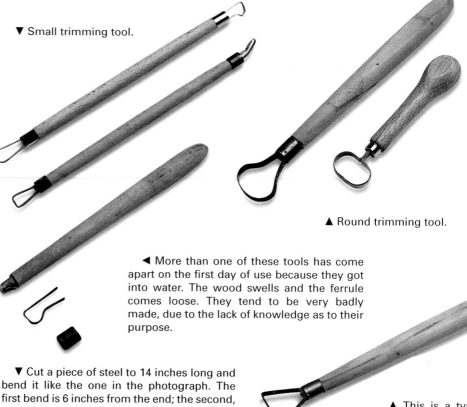

▼ Small trimming tool.

▲ Round trimming tool.

◄ More than one of these tools has come apart on the first day of use because they got into water. The wood swells and the ferrule comes loose. They tend to be very badly made, due to the lack of knowledge as to their purpose.

▼ Cut a piece of steel to 14 inches long and bend it like the one in the photograph. The first bend is 6 inches from the end; the second, at 1½ inches; the third at 6 inches; and the last at ½ inch. Insert the first piece into the hook-shaped one and squeeze the lower part together with the pliers. Before winding adhesive tape around it, make sure the cut is centered correctly. The handle should be about 2¾ inches long, but if you have a big hand, you can change the size. This tool should not be too large because the loop is not very strong.
We recommend that you make another tool whose second bend is made at 1 inch.

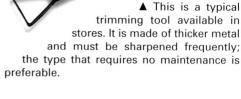

▲ This is a typical trimming tool available in stores. It is made of thicker metal and must be sharpened frequently; the type that requires no maintenance is preferable.

▼ Flexible ribs.

◄ Home-made trimming tool.

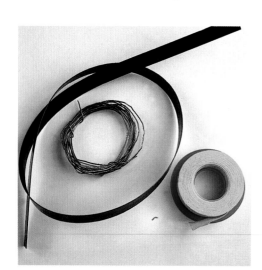

Flexible ribs

There are many of these tools to choose from, but not all of them work well. They must be thin and flexible, and the edges must be smooth. For making your own ribs, Swedish or German steel is the best.

▲ Materials required: copper wire or adhesive tape and strap iron ½ inch wide and ³/₆₄ inch thick.

◄ If you can't find these tools in your local shop, you can improvise with a piece of tin can. The problem is that bending the can may cause creases that leave marks on the clay. It all depends on the quality of the metal.

▲ In order to conform to the piece being worked on, ribs must be flexible and leave no marks on the clay. If the rib is repeatedly bent in this way, it will be free of creases.

► Since they are made of steel, these utensils rust easily and should occasionally be rubbed with sandpaper so that they don't increase in thickness or become stiff.

Cut pieces of flexible tin

You can cut pieces of flexible tin for use in hard-to-reach places. Any rough edges left from cutting may be smoothed with emery paper.

Half a pair of scissors and a chamois

Some ceramists use these items as a substitute for the needle tool. The chamois is used to smooth the edges of the pieces being thrown.

◄ Half a pair of scissors and leather strip.

Bats

The sizes of the bats vary according to the pieces to be thrown. They may be ten, fourteen, or eighteen inches in diameter by one-eighth-, one-half-, or three-quarters-of-an-inch thick. They are used as a support for throwing pieces that lose their shape when they are removed from the wheel head.

Chipboard bats

If these wooden supports get too wet, the wood swells, as you can see. Therefore, another type of wood should be used unless the

▼ Bats: red brick clay (A), plaster bat (B), and marine plywood bat (C).

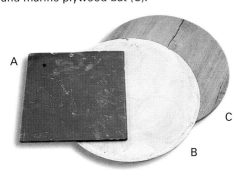

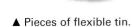

▲ Pieces of flexible tin.

▼ Chipboard stands.

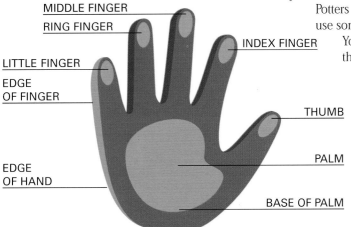

MIDDLE FINGER
RING FINGER
LITTLE FINGER
EDGE OF FINGER
EDGE OF HAND

INDEX FINGER
THUMB
PALM
BASE OF PALM

ceramist knows how to handle chipboard properly.

Heat gun

This tool is used to heat up and soften thermoplastic materials for bending. It is manufactured in two strengths.

It is used with the wheel for drying the clay in the chucks.

Once the dryer has been used, it should be left with the nozzle pointing upward, because it gets very hot. It must never be used for drying pieces of pottery because some types of clay may crack.

► The heat gun.

▲ Other materials: Basin for throwing, towel for drying your hands, plastic sheeting for covering pieces, and a sponge for cleaning the wheel.

Using your hands

The ceramist's most valuable tools are the hands. This book shows you how to throw with your hands and turn with tools.

Potters who don't turn their pieces use some tools for throwing.

You should be familiar with the different parts of your hand in order to know what parts to use in pressing on the clay to produce the desired shape.

*B*asic techniques for throwing are the procedures that are constantly repeated each time we use the potter's wheel. By grouping them into one section, we can examine each one of them in greater depth to make them easier to understand and keep them in mind while we're working.

The techniques explained are based on a way of working that is coherent unto itself and allows the reader to progress in a logical and orderly manner.

There are various ways of going about these techniques; all are valid as long as the procedure is followed correctly. Once they are clearly understood, and with some practice, they can be adapted to produce any desired results.

Basic
Techniques

Wedging the clay

Wedging the clay consists of mixing a quantity of clay to make it homogeneous.

The clay is worked on the wheel by exerting pressure. If a block of clay has not been wedged for some time, the inside will always be softer than the outside. When it is thrown and pressure is applied to it, it expands asymmetrically.

If we wedge the clay before throwing it to make it homogeneous, it will expand more consistently and will be easier for us to work. So for the project to turn out right, you'll have to wedge the clay you intend to work with.

There are two ways to wedge clay: manually or electrically.

Wedging the clay by hand

It's important for beginners to mix and wedge clay by hand in order to familiarize themselves with the ideal texture that clay should have for throwing on the wheel.

▶ **1.** If you have bought the clay, place a lump of it on the table. Peel off part of the plastic wrapper and cut off a four- to six-pound piece.

▲ **2.** Re-seal the wrapping before you begin wedging. Never leave it open; otherwise the clay will dry out.

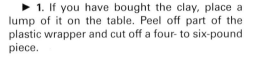

▲ **3.** If you already have the clay in the studio, take a piece and place your hands onto it in this position.

▲ **4.** Press the clay down against the work surface, squeezing it forward a little.

▲ **5.** Using your two middle fingers, roll it back toward you. You can do this using all your fingers, but beginners should try not to touch the clay too much, to keep it from drying out and cracking.

◀ **6.** Once you have turned the clay half-way over, place the palms of your hands onto it.

◀ **7.** Press down again and squeeze the clay forward, as you did in steps 4 and 5. Repeat this operation seven or eight times.

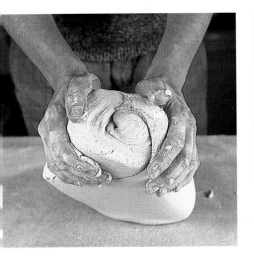

▲ **8.** Turn the clay on end.

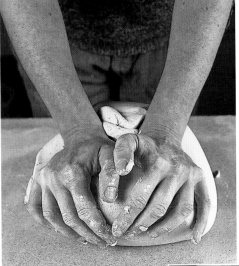
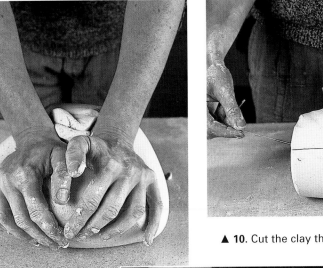

▲ **10.** Cut the clay through the middle.

▲ **9.** Press down again and squeeze the clay forward, as you did in steps 4 and 5. Repeat this operation seven or eight times.

◄ **11.** Turn over the part you've cut off and throw it forcefully onto the rest of the clay.

► **12.** Repeat once again steps 4 and 5, seven or eight times.

► **13.** Once you've done that several times, hold the clay in your hands wide-open and pound it down gently on the table, rolling it toward you. Do this as often as necessary to produce a cylinder.

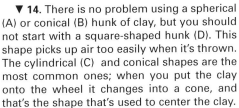

▼ **14.** There is no problem using a spherical (A) or conical (B) hunk of clay, but you should not start with a square-shaped hunk (D). This shape picks up air too easily when it's thrown. The cylindrical (C) and conical shapes are the most common ones; when you put the clay onto the wheel it changes into a cone, and that's the shape that's used to center the clay.

▲ **15.** Once you have finished wedging the clay, go over the work surface with a rib to remove any remaining clay. This way, the table will dry clean and free of leftover dry clay; that way it can't stick to soft clay the next time you wedge. If you scratch the table when you use the tool, hold it at a slight angle. You shouldn't use a wet dishcloth to wash the table, because unvarnished wood should not be treated with water.

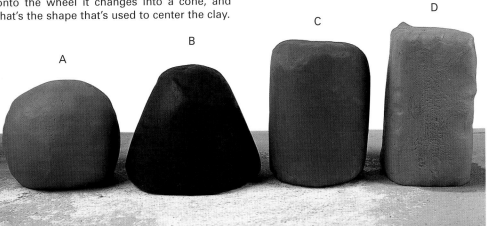

A

B

C

D

▲ **16.** Some potters mix the clay before they begin to wedge it. Press the clay into the table with both hands.

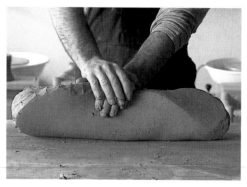

▲ **17.** Move your hands along the clay from one end to the other.

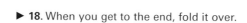

▶ **18.** When you get to the end, fold it over.

▲ **19.** Then begin process all over again. Three or four times is enough to mix clay that's not homogeneous.

▲ **20.** Next, wedge as explained earlier, without cutting it or turning it over. Finish the procedure by hitting one end with your hand to flatten it and by pressing the clay down against the table and turning it with the other, to form a cone.

▲ **21.** To conclude, spin the clay around as if it were a top so that the part that will contact the wheel head is compressed and free of cracks.

Defects that may emerge through wedging

Problems can arise during the wedging process, especially for the novice; but these problems are insignificant if you are aware of them and know how to fix them.

▶ **1.** When you press the clay down against the work surface and move your hands forward, don't exert too much pressure with the palm, or you'll leave hollows.

▶ **2.** When you turn the clay, these hollows will remain inside and trap air.

▲ **3.** If the clay gets too long while you are wedging it, change the position of your hands. You are probably pressing down too much in the center.

▼ **4.** It works well to open your hands a little more and use your ring and little fingers to keep the clay from squeezing out the ends.

▲ **5.** If the clay becomes filled with flaws or cracks when you wedge it, check its condition. It may either have become too hard, or it has been handled too much during the wedging process. The latter is a common fault among beginners.

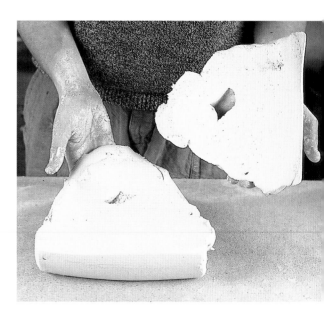

▲ **6.** If you cut the clay while wedging it and find air pockets, continue wedging until they disappear.

Wedging clay electrically

The pugmill is a machine that's used to wedge clay. If the clay placed inside this machine is in good condition, it will come out perfectly. But if it is too hard or too soft, it will have to be prepared beforehand. This machine doesn't modify the clay; what it does is mix it. That's why it's important to control the type of material you put into it.

The pugmill must be used often in order to prevent the clay left inside the machine from drying out. If this happens, you'll have to empty it without starting the motor. Otherwise you could burn out the motor.

Each time you want to change the type of clay, you will have to empty the machine completely.

If the pugmill is made of iron, you must take extra care when wedging porcelain, since rust stains the clay and can damage it.

◄ **1.** If you have just bought the clay you intend to wedge, you shouldn't encounter any problems: it can be placed directly in the machine. When you start to wedge, if you find that the clay is not uniformly moist, it will have to be cut into slices and mixed together thoroughly.

▶ **2.** Place a piece of clay into the top opening of the pugmill and press down hard on the handle so that it comes out through the nozzle.

▶ **3.** If the clay has difficulty going through the machine, add a few drops of water. If the clay you are wedging is a little dry, give it a little squirt of water. Once enough clay comes out the nozzle, cut off as much as you need.

The right amount of water needed for throwing

Where to sit

Regardless of the type of wheel you have chosen to use for throwing, you probably won't have any problems; but if you have a potter's wheel with a movable seat, it should be adjusted properly. You can get used to throwing while seated on a stool, but if you wish, you can use a chair. Even if you don't use the backrest while you are working, you can use it when you take a break.

► **1.** Place the chair in front of the potter's wheel so that when you are seated your elbows are about 8 inches above the wheel head. This allows you to work with your arms and not with your back. Spread your legs so that your knees are situated on the center line of the wheel head. If you don't feel comfortable, you can increase the distance between your elbows and the wheel head.

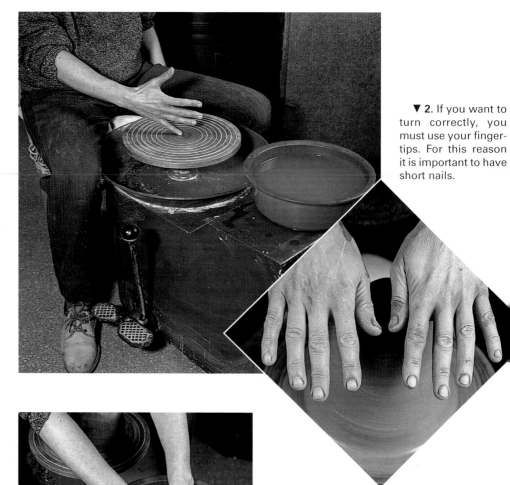

▼ **2.** If you want to turn correctly, you must use your fingertips. For this reason it is important to have short nails.

The right amount of water

Knowing the right amount of water is a little difficult for the beginner. This section presents a method that can help you use the right amount of water.

When you work you must wet your hands so that the clay slides and can be shaped. The water that's added to the clay as we work it with our hands turns into slip, a substance that allows our hands to slide over the clay.

If too much water is used, the clay absorbs it and becomes too soft. That makes it impossible to produce most pieces, and in many cases the clay will crack. Success with the potter's wheel comes from continually controlling the amount of water, and using only what's necessary.

▲ **1.** Place your hands in a basin containing enough water to cover the fingers.

► **2.** Then place them on the edge of the basin and rub the palms of your hands, but not your fingers, on the edge.

◄ **3.** Turn your hands over and place them in this position over the wheel head. If you move your hands toward the potter's wheel with your palms facing downward (as many beginners do), you will lose all the water you need for throwing.

► **4.** As you can see, the hands reach the wheel head with the right amount of water for throwing. The crucial thing here is not the position: this is just one way to get the amount of water you need. Any more than this is a hindrance to the work.

The first time you throw, you should repeat this process twice. The first time is to moisten the clay, and the second time is for throwing; this is the amount of water required for working.

◄ **5.** If you use more water than necessary, it will drip onto the lower tray of the wheel, assuming that your wheel has one. If it doesn't, the water will splash onto you, and you'll get covered with clay. Traditional potter's wheels do not have a tray, so you quickly learn to control the water.

▶ **6.** Control the water by placing your thumb ¹/₂ inch from the edge of the wheel head and your index finger against the rim at a right angle. If water falls into the tray, it means you are using too much water.

◄ **7.** In that case, don't add more water from the basin. Place your hands onto the wheel head so they fill with water, and direct it onto the lump of clay and use it as you work.

▶ **8.** If your hands are as clean as the ones in the photograph, you are using too much water; this will affect the moisture in the clay and detract from it.

▶ **9.** Your hands should be muddy, and the water that you use must turn into slip.

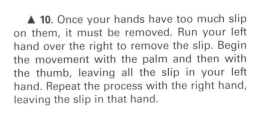

▲ **10.** Once your hands have too much slip on them, it must be removed. Run your left hand over the right to remove the slip. Begin the movement with the palm and then with the thumb, leaving all the slip in your left hand. Repeat the process with the right hand, leaving the slip in that hand.

▲ 11. Wipe the slip off against the rim of the basin. Don't put it in with the clay in the tray or you'll spoil it.

▶ 12. Don't use a sponge to clean your hands, since you will have to get used to throwing with them covered in slip rather than water. This practice may keep the beginner from successfully throwing some pieces.

◀ 13. If the tray fills up with water, stop the wheel and remove the water with a sponge before resuming work.

▶ 14. The clay should not be dry when you are throwing; otherwise it will be hard to use your hands.

◀ 15. The clay mass should shine; there should be slip on the wheel head, but there should not be too much water on the tray.

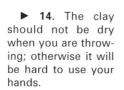

▶ 16. What should you do if you have too much water? Instead of throwing with water, throw with slip. Let a piece of clay dry; when it's dry, place it in water for at least three hours. Remove the excess water and stir the clay to make a paste. To avoid throwing with excess water, you should get used to throwing with slip.

Make sure the slip does not contain any lumps, or it will be harder to throw.

When you're done throwing, put the slip from the rim of the basin inside it, but don't pour out the water.

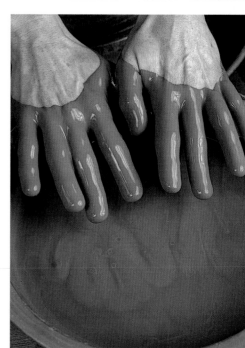

The first step in throwing ceramics is to center the clay. How do you do that? By placing the clay in the middle of the wheel head. How do you know if the clay is placed properly? By inspecting it from a distance while the wheel head is turning; if you can't tell if it's moving, the mass of clay appears to be of uniform shape. If it is not centered properly, the lump on the wheel appears to have different shapes.

How to place the clay on the wheel head

It's easy for a ceramist who has mastered the wheel to place the clay on the wheel head correctly; but a novice often has to move it around, even to the point of removing it from the wheel head.

Some ceramists prefer to prepare the wheel head before they place the clay on it. If you follow a few basic rules, the mass will stay put and not move.

▼ **3.** Before you place the clay on the wheel head, the bottom must be dull rather than shiny. If it's shiny, that means water is present; in that case, it will not stay put, and it may even slide around.

It may help to slam the clay forcefully onto the wheel with the motor turned off.

▶ **2.** Take a little clay from the lump without digging your fingers into it and place it onto the wheel head, starting in the center and going to about an inch from the edge as you press on it. If it doesn't adhere properly, it may be because the clay is not soft enough. In that case, wet the wheel head a little more with the clay on top of it and press again.

▶ **5.** Slam the lump of clay down once again onto the center.

◀ **1.** Turn on the wheel. Take some water with the right hand, (or the left, if you are left-handed) and wet the wheel head from the center to an inch from the edge.

◀ **4.** If it is far off center, repeat the operation. Cut the clay off at the level of the wheel head.

▲ **6.** Hit the clay with your hands until it is well centered. This is the easiest way to center it. Don't hit the base with the edges of your hands because it will turn into another shape that's more difficult to center.

If you place the clay randomly onto the wheel head, it will require more effort to center it.

Exercise for learning how to center

This exercise consists of learning how to draw up and lower the clay while keeping it on center.

The centering action consists of briefly pressing on the mass of clay, placing it in the center, keeping your hands motionless for a few seconds, and then slowly taking them away, so that the clay remains centered. Once the clay has been centered, if you do this too quickly and you're not an expert, it will come off center.

You should master this exercise before trying to make pieces, at least if you want to create uniform objects. If you cannot center the clay, try using softer clay.

▲ **1.** Place the clay on the wheel head and try to find a way to use your body for support to keep your hands still as you center. If the wheel permits it, lift one leg and rest against it.

▲ **2.** Another way is to use both legs for support.

▲ **3.** Get water by wetting your hands twice as you begin to work. The first time you wet the clay, and with the second you begin to turn, because the clay is dry and needs to slide.

▲ **4.** In the first place, the part of the clay touching the wheel head must be centered. Exert pressure on the clay with your fingers and the palm of your hand.

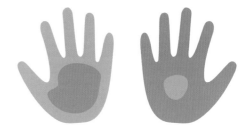

▲ The dark areas are the parts of the hands used in the previous photograph. The left hand supports the clay and presses it toward the center. The right hand gathers in all the clay and forces it toward the center and toward the left hand.

▼ **5.** Move your hands upward while applying pressure to the clay in the same way you did to the base.

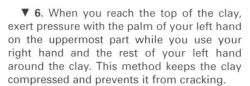

▼ **6.** When you reach the top of the clay, exert pressure with the palm of your left hand on the uppermost part while you use your right hand and the rest of your left hand around the clay. This method keeps the clay compressed and prevents it from cracking.

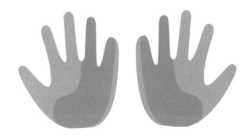

▲ Another way of centering is to apply pressure with the ring finger, the little finger, and the sides of both hands, all at the same time, attempting to gather all the clay from the base and move it to the center.

▲ You can also exert pressure with both hands at the same time as you try to find the center. The palms do the work, but the hollows of the hands are not used very much.

▲ **7.** It's important to apply enough pressure on the clay on top so that it stays solid. If the top cracks, the base will crack, especially when you make small pieces from a lump of clay. To keep the clay from sagging, apply a little more pressure to the side with your fingers, rather than with the palm of your hand on the top.

▲ **8.** Repeat steps 4, 5, and 6 to squeeze the clay farther up, until it takes on this shape. To master this exercise, you should learn how to squeeze in and push down the cone without disturbing its centering. Once you have achieved this—and not before—you will be ready to throw a piece.

▲ **9.** Push down on the cone while keeping it on center. Exert pressure on the top of the clay with your left hand, and hold your right hand around it to keep it from moving off center while you push down. You can swap hand positions if it's more comfortable for you.

▶ **10.** When pushing down on the clay, make sure it doesn't take on the shape of a mushroom. If the top of the mushroom merges with the base of the clay, it will trap air and possibly upset the centering.

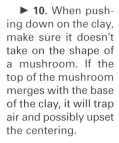

▲ **11.** To keep the clay from mushrooming, press on the sides of the clay at the same time you push down on the top. That way the clay lowers en masse rather than a little at a time.

▲ **12.** Push the cone down as much as possible until it has this shape.

▲ **13.** Squeeze the clay up without allowing it to come off center. When you squeeze it up, keep the top from forming a volcano shape, because that's another way to trap air.

▶ **14.** To avoid the volcano shape, squeeze the clay up by exerting pressure on both sides at the same time as the top. If you want to squeeze it up, the parts of the hands working on the sides must exert more pressure than the ones that are working on the top. If you want to push the clay down, the reverse applies.

▲ **15.** The cone must not be narrower in the middle than at the top; otherwise the clay will break during the centering process.

How to add more clay to the wheel head while you are working

It's not necessary to add clay as you did when you started throwing. You can use what's left on the base to attach the new clay.

If you want to clean the wheel head because you are going to use a different type of clay, repeat the process you did when you began throwing.

▶ **1.** While practicing centering, it's easy to run out of clay to work with. In that case, add some more.

▲ **2.** Dig with your fingers into the clay remaining on the wheel head to create grooves; this removes slip from the top.

◀ **3.** Forcefully throw another lump down on top. This clay will serve as a base for adding more. If the clay you intend to use doesn't have the same hardness as the previous type, it's better to remove the remaining clay from the wheel head before placing another type on top.

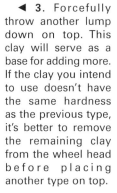

◀ **4.** Whenever you cut a lump of clay off the wheel head, leave the remainder so that the next lump you put on will adhere properly.

How to center or move the clay up according to the piece being thrown

The clay needs to be centered in one way or another, depending on the type of piece you want to throw.

If you want to make small pieces, it's better to work with lumps. If the piece you want to make is narrow and tall and holds its shape when you remove it from the wheel, it should be thrown directly on the wheel head. But if the piece you want to make is wide and low, or if you have problems when you take it off the wheel because of the clay you are using, you will have to work on a bat.

Working with lumps

Potters use lumps to produce the majority of their small and medium-sized pieces, sometimes even dinner plates. But depending on the material used, only small pieces can be made. This approach keeps us from having to center a small piece of clay every time.

All the small pieces that can be made from lumps and that don't lose their shape when you take them off the wheel, or that regain their shape after being left for a while, must be made using this procedure.

▼ **1.** To make a small piece, you will have to center the clay in the form of a cone with a narrow top. With your hands around the clay to steady them, stick your thumb into the top.

▲ **2.** Keep you thumb inside the hole until it's completely centered.

▲ **3.** Use your index fingers to press against the inside edge of the hole and open up the clay. Keep the fingers that are outside the hole about an inch below the bottom of the hole you have made. Otherwise the piece of clay will not have a base, and when you cut the piece off, it will have a hole in it. The thumbs work the other side of the cone and are placed in a manner similar to that of the middle fingers.

◄ **4.** Choose the clay you want to use to make the piece. This will be the only clay you will work with; therefore, you can only make a piece about the size of a liquor glass.

◄ **5.** How do you proceed? Use your hand—except for the thumb—to support the clay you have selected. Insert your thumb into the mass by pressing toward the center and upward at the same time. If you continue pressing, the result will be a bowl with thick walls.

◄ **6.** If you want to make a slightly larger piece, insert your thumb farther into the cone; that way you can grab more clay to work with. The rest of the procedure is the same as already described.

Working directly on the wheel head

There are four ways or stages of opening up the clay directly on the wheel head. They are explained in the following passages.

Opening up a small amount of clay with a flat base

When you work directly on the wheel head, it is necessary to center the entire mass correctly, specifically the area in direct contact with the wheel head, as this is the most difficult part to center.

It is important to use all the clay to make the piece. If a thick layer of clay is left at the bottom, you haven't made the opening correctly.

With this quantity of clay you can make a cylinder, and since there's not much clay, you can work with your hands linked together by the thumbs, with one hand on the inside and the other on the outside throughout the process. The main difficulty in making this opening is centering the base.

► **3.** With index fingers inside and thumbs on the outside, apply pressure to the clay in the base so that it is evenly distributed along the wall. Although your whole left hand is on the inside, work only with your index finger. Now work on the flat base and apply pressure to level it out and reduce it to a little less than an inch in thickness.

▲ **1.** Center the clay. Insert your thumb and do not remove it until the hole is completely centered.

▲ **2.** Insert both hands, exerting pressure toward the wheel head and yourself while you open up the mass. The pressure should be applied with the fingertips until they reach about an inch from the wheel head.

▼ **4.** Before pulling the clay upward, the base must be flat and the walls must have the same thickness. This is the opening that's used for making a cylinder.

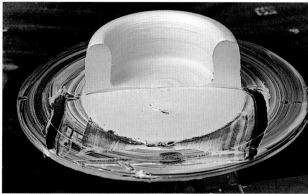

Opening up clay with a curved base

It's appropriate to differentiate from the outset the two types of bases: flat and curved. Both are useful.

If this type of opening is not considered from the outset, you may discover that you have no clay left in the base.

► **1.** Center the clay by pressing down toward the wheel head with your thumbs, and at the same time toward the center with the rest of your hand.

▲ **3.** Press the clay on the base with the index finger of your right hand to eliminate any thick spots in the base.

▼ **5.** Since the interior shape must be the same as the exterior, apply pressure to the outside in order to thin down the base.

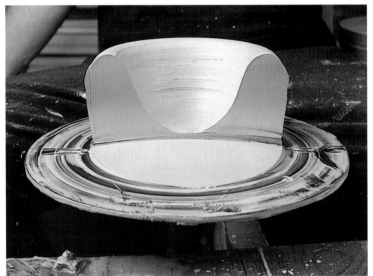

▲ **2.** Open up the mass by applying pressure perpendicularly toward the wheel head to create a thickness of about an inch. Once your hands are placed in the center, apply pressure in an upward direction, not parallel to the base, and a little toward yourself, to open up the base.

◄ **4.** This is what the clay would look like if we were to cut it open at this stage.

▲ **6.** This is what the clay would look like if we opened it up at this stage. This is the shape the clay should have for making a bowl, before the clay is pulled up.

If the base is not opened up correctly from the outset and you don't have much experience with the wheel, it will be much more difficult later on.

Opening up clay when your hands must work separately

You should gradually increase the amount of clay you work with in order to resolve problems of opening up and centering. When working with more material, your hands must work separately, and that's a little more difficult.

This opening is not more difficult than the previous one because it's more complicated, but because you will have to exert more pressure, and you'll have to keep your hands immobile independently of one another.

▲ **1.** Center the clay, making sure that the bottom is completely centered. Then insert your thumb.

▲ **2.** Now insert both hands, pressing downward and opening up the hole. Work the base by pressing with your fingertips down to about an inch from the wheel head.

▲ **3.** Use your fingertips to apply more pressure and continue opening the base.

The inch of clay left in the base at the beginning is now reduced to about ³/₄ inch as you apply pressure to flatten the base. Now you'll learn how to open up the clay so you can make tall pieces later on.

▲ **4.** Once the base has been flattened, press on the extra clay at the bottom of the side. This corresponds to step 3 on page 39, but since we are working with more clay and applying more pressure, your hands work independently.

▲ **5.** It's a good idea to repeat the exercise with a little more clay. To avoid applying more force than is necessary, you should position the clay by hitting it with your hands.

▲ **6.** Center the clay, insert first one thumb and then the other, and open up the lump.

▶ **7.** Insert both hands to within an inch of the base and work with your fingertips, just as you did in step 3.

▲ **8.** Exert pressure on the clay at the bottom and the side, just as you did in step 4. Since there's more clay, you'll need to use more force. Now flatten the base until it is ³/₄ inch thick.

Opening up the clay from the top

In order to make a tall, narrow piece, you will have to center the clay high rather than low; that way you'll save a lot of unnecessary trouble drawing up and lowering of the clay. You should master the previous exercise before attempting this one; if you try this one first, you won't make the base correctly, because it's harder to get to.

This method of opening up the clay tends to leave pieces of clay stuck to your hand. If this happens, just remove the clay. Whether or not the clay sticks depends on the slip you have created, the hardness of the clay, and the amount of pressure exerted when you insert your hand into the clay. This is the quickest way to make big, tall pieces.

◄ **1.** Stack several lumps of clay on the wheel head of the same size that you would normally wedge.

► **2.** To keep water from getting into the joints between the pieces, and to save effort in centering the clay, hit the pieces to position them correctly.

► **3.** Wet your hands and the clay, and begin centering it at the base.

► **4.** Place your hands around the uppermost part of the block, applying pressure simultaneously to the top and the sides. If you exert more pressure to the walls than on the top, the block will rise; if you do the opposite, the block will lower.

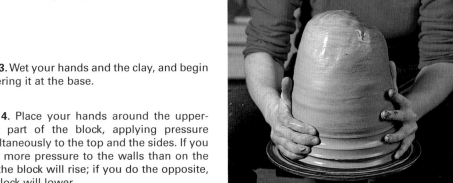

▲ **5.** First insert one thumb and then the other.

▲ **6.** Now insert both hands to enlarge the hole.

▲ **7.** Place a fistful of lump-free slip from the tray into the hole.

▲ **8.** Now insert a closed fist inside the hole and force it downward toward the wheel head.

► **9.** If your hand cannot reach far enough into a large piece, you will have to stand so that the clay is at your side. Once you've reached down within an inch of the base, work with your hand in this position to open up the hole.

► **10.** Once the clay has been opened up, the inside of the piece must be worked flat. Apply pressure to the base of the wall and squeeze the clay upward.

Working on a bat to make a low, wide piece

Up to this point, the clay placed on the wheel head was tall and narrow because of the pieces being made. Now we'll center a low, wide lump of clay for this type of piece.

Depending on how the clay is worked, when you open it up to make a low, wide piece, parts of the base touching the wheel head may not have any clay. If that's the case, the opening and the position of the clay will have to be modified.

These types of pieces tend to lose their shape when they're removed from the wheel, so they should be worked on a stand.

▲ **1.** Place the clay as wide as possible and center it low.

Exert pressure with your thumbs and the palms of your hands toward the wheel head, and at the same time, use your remaining fingers to press toward the center of the wheel.

The clay will take on a more or less broad shape, depending on the force applied in one direction or another.

▲ **2.** Press down with the palm of your right hand from the center toward the wheel head and the outside edge; keep your left hand on the edge to steady the clay.

▲ **3.** Another way of opening up the clay is to apply pressure with your fingertips from the center to the edge, and at the same time in the direction of the wheel head.

▶ **4.** Once you have worked the base to create the desired thickness, insert the middle finger, ring finger, and little finger of your right hand underneath the rim of the piece and raise the piece by applying pressure while your other fingers work on the inside.

◀ **6.** You can also open up a low, wide piece by inserting your hands into the mass and pressing toward the wheel head, as indicated.

▲ **5.** With the index finger of your right hand hooked around the thumb on the outside, and with the left hand on the inside (except for the thumb, which links both hands together), press down on the clay at the base to thin it out.

▶ **7.** Press the clay toward yourself. Depending on how much force is used and the hardness of the clay, this type of opening in such a thick piece of clay can create a double rim at the top. This should disappear as the work progresses, but if it doesn't, cut off the mouth and flatten it.

Bats

Pieces that lose their shape when they are removed from the wheel head, either because the clay isn't strong enough or because their mouths are too wide, must be thrown on a stand.

There are many types of stands: solid wood, chipboard, plaster, and fired ceramic, all of which are porous.

All pieces thrown on stands come away cleanly when dry. Some take longer than others, depending on the thickness, the type of clay, and the room temperature. So if you have to touch a piece before it loosens from the stand, you will have to separate it by cutting the base.

It's a good idea to cut pieces off while the bats are still in place on the wheel head, so that the cut is completely even and parallel to the wheel.

How to prepare the base for placing a bat

There is no need to make a clay base to install a bat on the wheel head. If the clay you're working with is hard, it may not stick well to the bat; since it's porous, it may absorb part of the moisture from the clay.

If the clay you're using is very soft, it may deform excessively when it's thrown forcefully onto the bat. In any case, the base often has to be adjusted.

▶ **3.** Make a groove by pressing with the index finger of your right hand.

▼ **5.** Turn the wheel off and make three marks with the side of your hand.

▲ **1.** Center the clay low and wide. Flatten it out by pressing with the palm of your right hand, working from the center to the rim of the wheel head while keeping the mass centered with your left hand. If the bat you're using is bigger than the wheel head, you'll have to make a base that covers the entire wheel head.

▲ **6.** If the clay you have put onto the bat is fairly hard, wet the plaster on the side that will contact the clay before placing it on the wheel head. That way the plaster won't absorb moisture from the clay and will be attached properly.

▲ **2.** Now make a hole in the clay down to the wheel head.

▲ **4.** Make another groove parallel to the first one. If the clay has lost its shape and the base is no longer flat, you'll have to fix it. Since it's very difficult to make it perfectly parallel to the original groove, it should be made slightly deeper in the middle than at either edge, as if it were a gutter.

▼ **7.** Place the bat on top of the clay base and try to center it. With the wheel turned on and your left hand placed in the center of the bat, hit it with your right hand whenever it wobbles, until it is completely centered. Plaster bats work well because the piece comes loose by itself.

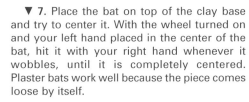

▲ **8.** If the bat is made of wood and is lighter than plaster, you can pick it up by the rim with your hands and slide it until it's centered. This procedure doesn't work with plaster bats, since clay quickly sticks to the plaster and the bat can't be moved for centering. You have to control excess moisture with these types of bats to avoid damaging them.

▼ **11.** When you're throwing on glazed tiles, keep your wrists arched upward so you don't get caught by the edges. These bats are cheap and adhere well, since they're grooved on one side.

▲ **9.** If the bat you're using is smaller than the wheel head, the base must be a little smaller than the support.

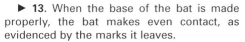

▲ **12.** If the base is not made properly, the bat will be supported only in the center. In this case the bat can break loose while you're working.

▶ **13.** When the base of the bat is made properly, the bat makes even contact, as evidenced by the marks it leaves.

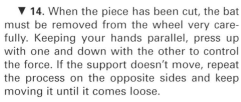

▼ **14.** When the piece has been cut, the bat must be removed from the wheel very carefully. Keeping your hands parallel, press up with one and down with the other to control the force. If the support doesn't move, repeat the process on the opposite sides and keep moving it until it comes loose.

▲ **10.** Once you have situated the bat, hit it in the center, not on the sides, to even it out. Don't worry if it's not completely parallel to the wheel head; when it's time to turn the piece, center the mouth and flatten the base so that they are parallel to one another.

◀ When you're working with a lot of clay and you want to make very large, heavy pieces, it's best to use a bat that's larger than the wheel head and has a fixture on the underside that allows it to be set directly on the wheel without having to put clay in between. It's common to use these types of bat when making very large pieces.

▲ Some supports have lugs on the underside that fit into holes in the wheel head. These elements must be custom made for each type of potter's wheel.

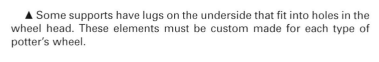

Turning with chucks

Turning is the process applied to a piece the day after it has been thrown, when the clay is harder. A knowledge of turning is basic to throwing all kinds of pieces on the wheel to obtain any desired shape. The secret of turning consists of counteracting with the left hand the force that is applied by a tool held in the right hand; that way the piece remains centered throughout the job.

There are two main ways of turning: turning only the base, and turning the entire piece.

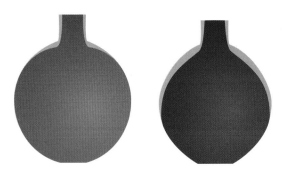

▲ During the turning process a single shape can be worked in different ways to modify its shape. If the part of the body that meets the neck is turned and the base is reduced at the same time, the piece will be become rounder in shape.

▶ Pieces that are turned all over are valued for their finish, and their shape is refined in the turning process. Depending on the clay used, the weight of the piece is reduced during this process.

◀ But if the piece is turned along its wall, it becomes more elongated in shape. This is how you refine the shape you want.

▼ Some pieces can't be thrown on a wheel if they are not turned. A knob shape cannot be narrowed too much at the neck after it's thrown because it can break easily.

◀ Pieces that are made thin are turned only at the base. You can leave the marks your hands made in the throwing process, and once they're in place the weight and shape of the piece are set.

These types of pieces are worked when they've dried more than ones that are to be polished completely.

▼ It's a good idea to let it dry, and when the clay is harder, the neck can be narrowed and adjusted to the desired shape.

▼ You can achieve totally different results from the same shape. These pieces can be obtained only by turning.

Chucks

Chucks are clay supports that are made on the wheel to hold thrown pieces when they're being turned. The purpose of the chuck is to hold any thrown piece so you can work on it while it's still moist. Potters rarely use them nowadays because they seldom turn their wares. They usually make the same types of traditional objects that don't need turning. Ceramists, on the other hand, make different kinds of pieces that do require turning.

Due to the variety of pieces that can be turned, successful use of the chuck depends on understanding the relationship between it and the object to be turned, and on fashioning the right chuck for each piece.

Characteristics of chucks

The chucks shown in this book can be made with the same clay used for throwing the piece.

After making the chuck, use a heat gun to dry the part of it that will come into direct contact with the piece, so that the clay of the chuck won't stick to the piece and damage it.

▶ Dry only the part of the chuck that will support the piece, with the wheel turned on. Ten seconds is usually enough to dry it. If you dry the entire chuck, you won't be able to reuse the clay to modify the chuck. If you dry it too much, the piece will slide as it's being turned. Moisture and the shape of the contact surface between the piece and the chuck are what make the two of them adhere correctly.

When does a piece have the right moisture level for turning?

A piece should not be turned while it's still very moist. Pieces usually dry first at the mouth, and finally at the foot.

The color of a piece changes in the drying process. To turn a piece successfully you must handle it at the right moment.

Turning a bowl or a cylinder

The chuck used to turn the outer surface of a bowl or a cylinder must be in the shape of a cone. It may be solid or hollow, depending on the size of the piece you're making. Solid cones are used for small pieces, and whenever you want enough resistance for the work to remain centered throughout the process.

The top of the cone must be flat, rather than rounded. If it were round, it would have the same shape as the bowl and would stick to it.

The following exercise shows in detail how to make a chuck.

▲ A piece has the right amount of moisture when you can hold it by the mouth without deforming it. Why do we need to hold it by the mouth? Because when we turn a piece, we hold it by the mouth to center it and handle it. If the piece is damp, it may lose its shape; but if it's too dry, it will be difficult to thin it with the tool.

▲ Some pieces have a small mouth and dry easily, but that does not mean they are ready to turn. That's the case with certain pots. With these pieces, press your thumb hard against the base. If the clay moves easily, it's still too moist and should be left to dry a little longer.

▲ **1.** Center the clay perfectly in the shape of a cone and flatten the top. Once it's centered, remove the slip with a rib.

◄ **3.** Before you pick the piece up, dry your hands with a towel to avoid damaging it.

▲ **2.** If the top of the cone is not flattened enough in the centering process, it can be cut off with a needle tool; this will eliminate unnecessary work.

▼ **6.** Remove the mark with the rib, taking care not to leave holes in the clay. Air holes are an indication that you have applied too much pressure.

◄ **4.** Place the piece over the chuck and center it. In the case of a cylinder, you can support it on any part of the cone.

▲ **5.** Remove the piece from the chuck and check to see that the mark it has left is centered.

▶ **7.** Use the heat gun to dry only the area of the chuck that will support the piece. You previously placed the piece onto the chuck to see where they would contact one another.

▼ **9.** Cross your thumbs on the other side so that the bowl is cradled in your hands. If the piece jumps off the chuck it will be easier to catch before it falls.

Centering consists of raising the piece ½ inch over the wheel head, then lowering it again, allowing it to slide over your thumbs and index or middle fingers, which are kept in place below the mouth. This procedure is repeated several times until the mouth of the bowl is parallel to the wheel head.

▲ **8.** A bowl must be supported by the mouth and the upper circumference of the cone. Place the bowl upside down over the chuck. Turn the wheel on and center it with your middle fingers held below the mouth.

◀ **10.** It's also possible to center the piece by placing your index fingers below the mouth. To make the chuck correctly, there must be enough space to place your fingers in this position.

How do we know when piece is placed correctly? Look at it at the level of the mouth. If you cannot see clearly, stand back a little from the wheel. Once the piece has been centered, you can begin turning.

Modifying the chuck when you can't center the cone

Never turn unless the chuck or the piece is completely centered. If you don't observe this rule, the turned pieces may end up lopsided.

▲ **2.** Cut off a strip of clay, leaving the top completely centered.

▶ **1.** If you haven't mastered the centering technique, try centering with a long needle tool. Hold it tightly with both hands, brace your arms against your body, and insert the needle at an angle.

▶ **3.** When you cut off the top, don't alter the cone, or it will be difficult to center the piece.

▼ **4.** Continue cutting the wall to restore the cone shape. This will be difficult if the needle you are using is uneven, or if the handle is too small.

▶ **5.** Finally, go over it with the rib to restore the cone shape. As you run the tool over the chuck, don't let it sink in and create bumps, since they are difficult to remove. To avoid this, hold the rib at an angle rather than perpendicular to the chuck.

When you have trouble centering pieces on chucks

If you can't center the piece by the mouth, find out what's wrong. This problem occurs only when you center small pieces.

► 1. Once you've made the chuck, if the piece sticks tight and there's not enough room to use your fingers to center it, you need to make a narrower cone. This piece is not gripped by the mouth of the cone but by the walls. If you manage to center it perfectly onto this chuck, that's fine, but this is usually difficult with certain types of pieces.

▲ 2. This chuck was modified excessively with the needle tool, making it difficult to center the bowl correctly. If this happens, you need to modify the chuck, making another one that's narrower and completely conical.

▼ 3. It is difficult to center pieces on such small chucks.

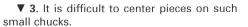
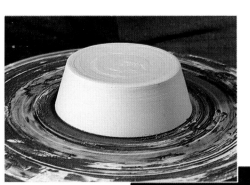

◄ 4. When positioning the piece, there is not enough room to use your hands to center it.

► 5. Pieces should be held on the chuck by the upper part of the cone, and inside the mouth of the piece. If the chuck grips too far inside the piece, when you try to work on the mouth, the piece comes off center because it is not held securely. In this case, cut off a piece of the chuck until the mouth of the piece is the same size as the upper part of the cone.

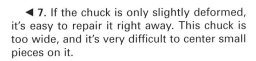

► 6. Every time you take a piece off the chuck, fix the wall if it's deformed. If you replace the piece without repairing the chuck, it will not be fully centered, and it will turn out lopsided.

It's important not to let the chuck become too deformed, or it will be too difficult to repair. If the clay is very soft, it should be dried out a little more with the heat gun so it doesn't lose its shape so much.

◄ 7. If the chuck is only slightly deformed, it's easy to repair it right away. This chuck is too wide, and it's very difficult to center small pieces on it.

► 8. Apply pressure on the deformed area with your right index finger and it will smooth out easily. If this happens frequently, dry the contact area a little more. You should note the difference between this chuck and the one in step 5, page 48.

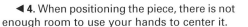
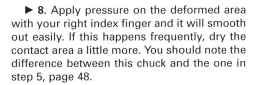

What do you do when the mouths of the pieces aren't the same size?

When this happens, you have to keep modifying the chuck. It's a good idea to start turning the pieces with the smallest mouths and progress to the larger ones. This generally occurs with bowls, not with cylinders.

How to turn the inside of a bowl and a cylinder

Bowls are usually turned on the inside. If a bowl was badly thrown or the chuck has damaged it, repair it; otherwise, smooth the interior, and finish by turning the mouth. With cylinders, the inside is not turned; only the mouth is turned, and it's repaired if damaged by turning.

▲ 1. If you have to turn a piece with a slightly larger mouth, cut off a piece of the cone. This is why it's a good idea to make taller chucks: you can modify them as you work.

▲ 2. When repairing the chuck, excess clay should be piled to one side, apart from the clay that still needs to be turned. The clay from the chuck can be reused, but the clay from the turning needs to be completely dry before it can be reused. That way the clay doesn't get ruined.

▲ 3. It doesn't matter if the cone doesn't have totally straight walls, like this one. If they are very curved, though, when you cut off pieces to turn vessels with larger mouths, the chucks may occasionally break. That's why it's a good idea to make straight walls.

▲ 1. Modify the chuck you have used to turn the exterior. Push the clay down and open up a hole.

▲ 2. Next, push your hands inside and open it up, working down to the wheel head.

▲ 3. Make the edge thicker so that later on you can cut it at an angle to the wheel.

▲ 4. Use the long needle tool to cut the upper part parallel to the wheel.

▶ 5. Cut the inside edge at an angle to the base.

▼ 6. Cut the outer edge to ensure that it's perfectly centered and to remove the slip. If it's right, it can be left as it is, because the outside is not going to be used. Next apply the heat gun only to the area that will hold the piece.

▲ 7. If you're turning a bowl, hold it against the chuck at any point around the outer wall. Take the piece by the mouth and place your index fingers over the edge and slide it into the center. The interior of the chuck should never be bowl shaped, as it would then grip the entire wall and damage it. It should be held only along a line no greater than ¼ inch wide.

▲ 8. A cylinder should be secured to the chuck by the outer circumference of the base. When turning a cylinder, it only needs to be inserted an inch or two inside the chuck. The centering process is the same as above.

▲ 9. If the piece to be turned is a medium-sized bowl, make a hole in the chuck down to the base to avoid having to work with so much clay. In this case, you have to cut the outside edge of the chuck because that's where it will grip the bowl.

▲ 10. If possible, the same chuck can be used when you turn the inside of the bowl.

How to make a chuck for turning a vase

A chuck for turning vases must be cylindrical and thick. A hole must be made down to the wheel; only a third of the piece to be turned will be placed inside the chuck.

Ideally, you can use the same chuck to turn the upper and lower parts of the piece. If necessary, reduce the diameter of the base slightly before starting to turn.

Vases with long, narrow necks require tall chucks, and generally need modifying to turn the pieces on both sides.

▲ 1. It's a good idea to place a large piece of clay on the wheel head, because if the clay is soft, the thickness of the walls will make up for it, preventing the chuck from losing its shape in the turning process. Open up a hole in the clay, working down to the wheel head, and adjust the walls.

▶ 4. And then the upper edge.

◀ 5. Then also cut the inside edge. That's how to make sure the chuck is completely centered. If it's not cut properly, repeat the process. Steps 3, 4, and 5 can be carried out in any order.

▲ 2. Make the mouth thicker.

▲ 3. Cut away the outside edge.

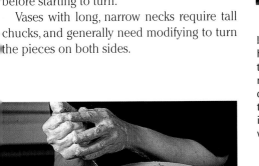

◀ 6. Use the heat gun to dry out the part of the inside edge that will grip the piece.

▶ 7. The chuck should be usable for turning the piece on both sides, so center it first upside down, remove the rough edge, reduce the diameter of the base, and turn the piece over. Then begin to turn the upper part, starting at the mouth.

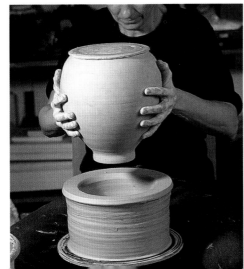

How to turn a centerpiece or bowl

A chuck for turning bowls must have the same diameter as the mouth of the piece being turned, and should be held by the mouth so the piece doesn't lose its shape.

Don't turn if the piece becomes deformed, or it will be damaged in the process.

▲ **1.** Center the clay wide and low and open a hole.

▲ **2.** Press down toward the wheel head and toward yourself.

▲ **3.** Open it up wider than the wheel head. You need to turn a piece with a diameter larger than that of the wheel head.

▲ **4.** Make the mouth thick.

▲ **5.** Cut off the outside edge.

▲ **6.** Then cut away the top.
▼ **9.** And place the piece on the chuck.

▲ **7.** And also the inside edge.

▲ **8.** Use the heat gun to dry the area that will contact the piece.

▼ **10.** Slide it into the center by holding it by the mouth. Since this piece has a very wide base, the same chuck cannot be used for turning the inside. It therefore needs to be modified by opening it up more once the outside is finished. This is a simple operation: just increase the diameter of the chuck, cut off the edges as usual, and place it right-side up.

How to turn a plate

You can use the same chuck to turn both sides of a plate, provided you take into account the following rule:

You can turn the outside and inside of the piece by rotating it continuously as you adjust the thickness. The foot is worked on last, unless it's the same size as the center hole; in this case it should be inserted into the hole to avoid damaging it.

The thickness of the piece is usually adjusted by working on both sides and finishing on the inside of the piece. Let it dry right-side up on a support for a day, and the next day form the foot on the base, finish the piece, and leave it to dry upside down.

Large pieces cannot be turned in one day.

► **1.** Center the clay low and wide on the wheel and flatten it.

◄ **2.** Cut the top nearly flat; but since that's practically impossible, cut on a slight angle toward the inside, as if it were a gutter. If the angle is too steep, it won't properly grip the piece being turned.

▼ **3.** Cut away the outside edge. Here it's not necessary to cut the inside edge because it's very small and won't be used.

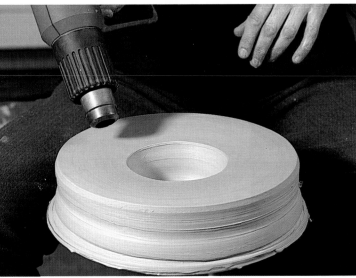

▲ **4.** Dry the entire surface. During the turning process, if the surface becomes too dry, it can be moistened a little with the fingers, because if the chuck is not damp, the piece can move around easily.

► **5.** Center the piece mouth down, and then mouth up.

It usually doesn't move if the chuck and the piece are sufficiently moist, because the tool is pressed downward toward the wheel. You'll notice how the piece rests on the chuck and leaves marks. Modify the chuck if the piece is not properly supported.

Parallel rims and bases

For vases or utilitarian pieces, it's traditional to finish the rim parallel to the base. Not all cultures follow the same tradition. The Japanese have developed a philosophy on the subject. In Japan, the finish of certain rims is related to the landscape, so the more irregularities (or mountains, in their view) the better, with the most complex pieces having up to five.

In the work shown throughout this book, we always emphasize rims that are parallel to the bases and pieces that are centered and straight, but this does not mean that there aren't other valid systems for finishing pieces.

Cutting rims with the needle tool

The only method of cutting rims shown in this book uses the needle tool, since that's the most accurate way. If the rims are not perfect, it will be impossible to make the pieces described in the exercise "Pots with lids," pages 142 to 157.

▶ **3.** Wait until the needle cuts through the wall of the piece and has completed a full turn.

▶ **4.** If the piece is a large one, lift both hands quickly; you will be left with a ring of clay. If the piece is small, it's not necessary to raise the hands so quickly. This is why this step is not shown with the preceding piece.

▼ **6.** If the piece has an uneven rim, cut away a thicker strip so it will come off in one piece; otherwise it can fall onto the piece and damage it.

▲ **1.** Hold the needle parallel to the piece to be cut. If it's held straight against the piece and the piece is off center, it will cut in too suddenly and may spoil it.

▲ **7.** When you cut the mouth, observe the thickness of the wall. If it's too thick and the piece is properly thrown, it requires further thinning. When you cut such a large piece, it's easy for the strip to break under its own weight.

▲ **2.** The tip of the needle is slowly inserted into the piece.

▼ **5.** Pinch the fingers to gather the rough edges left after cutting. The thumb and index finger control the thickness of the wall and remove the roughness from the inside and outside edges of the mouth. Use the index finger of your right hand to flatten the mouth, but without pressing down hard toward the base, so you don't deform the edge. The other fingers do nothing.

Cutting the base

The base of a piece is cut parallel to the wheel. Since it's not always possible to do this correctly, it's essential to cut the rim parallel to the wheel first, so it can be used as a reference point. When you're turning and the piece is centered mouth down, you return to the initial position of the piece, again centering the rim parallel to the base.

If the base was not cut straight, the initial position of the piece can be reestablished by flattening it parallel to the rim and working on it completely centered.

The base can be cut in two ways: off the hump, or directly on the wheel head.

Cutting pieces off the hump

The base of a piece formed on the hump is cut with cotton thread that has a clothespin at only one end.

The cutting action should be quick. If you're not experienced at it, you should reduce the speed of the wheel before cutting.

▶ **1.** Once the piece to be cut off is finished, mark the base with the tip of your thumb, holding it parallel to the wheel to make a straight line.

▼ **3.** Move your left hand parallel to the base and toward you, and release the end of the thread. If the hand doesn't move parallel, the cut will be uneven.

Cutting directly on the wheel

Pieces can be cut directly on the wheel, either stopped or in motion, using metal wire or nylon line. The finer the cutting wire, the less clay will be left on the base.

There shouldn't be too much water on the wheel before cutting the piece; otherwise the water that gets under it will produce a suction effect. If this happens, the pieces can't be removed from the wheel head without deforming them.

It's better to cut large pieces with the wheel in motion.

▼ **4.** As it winds around, the thread pulls the right hand a little toward the center; the same hand then pulls the thread back out, cutting the piece off.

▼ **2.** If you cut with the wheel in motion, use the method described above. This produces better results, since less clay is left on the wheel head.

If you're afraid of breaking the piece because it's very large, with the wheel turned off, use the thread to cut one-third of the way through the bottom of the piece. Then turn the wheel on, and with your hands held as taut as possible, finish cutting the base. This type of piece can't be removed by hand without losing its shape.

◀ **1.** It's easy to cut the piece while the wheel is stationary: just stretch a piece of thread the size of the piece and pass it under the piece, holding it very taut.

▲ **2.** Before cutting, wind the thread onto the wood so that you have a length just twice the diameter of the piece to be cut. If the thread is too long, it will wrap around the cone and spoil the work. Hold it taut and position it at the marked area around the base, cutting into the clay ¼ inch.

▼ **5.** Take the bowl quickly with your left hand and hold it by the base. If this is done correctly, it will recover its original shape when you put it onto a bat. This is done so quickly that when I did it for this sequence, the piece fell onto the floor. So you can understand how rapidly this is done, we show another piece. If the thread is pulled sharply with the left hand when you cut, the piece will remain on the wheel, provided, of course, that the speed is not too great.

▼ **3.** Once the piece has been cut off, dry your hands thoroughly on a towel so they won't slip, and remove it from the wheel. Make sure you don't sink your fingers in; rather, keep your hands opened flat so that the weight is evenly distributed. Place it on a flat support and let it dry.

Reusing clay

The basic material used in throwing is clay. If you want to work well, you must learn how to conserve clay.

Whenever you have clay that is too moist or too dry, a good way to get the right degree of hardness is to mix it; that way you keep the clay from losing its plasticity.

When an exercise doesn't turn out right, check out the clay you're using. In some cases you need to use slightly softer clay—for example, when you're having trouble centering it. In other cases, slightly harder clay is called for, such as when you don't have much experience and you work the clay for a long time as you throw a bowl off the hump.

You should never use clay that was used the previous day. It's better to use half old and half fresh, as beginners tend to ruin quite a bit of clay.

These ideas will help you keep in mind the quality of the clay, since it changes as it's worked, and it's hard to know the right amount of hardness.

▶ **2.** Clay should not be thrown into the basin, since it loses plasticity as it gets wetter and drier.

What to do when the clay is too wet to throw

If the clay you have used for throwing is too moist and cannot be mixed with another drier clay, let it dry out some.

Storing clay when the job is done

The way in which you store the clay depends on how you worked it. If the clay you bought is hard, it can be mixed with soft clay; if soft, let it dry so it will be in good condition when it's time to use it. When mixing hard and soft clay, it's better to cut it into slices and

▶ **1.** After centering, there will be some slip on the edge of the bowl and some lumpy slip on the wheel. If you have already made another piece, there will also be some small pieces of clay.

The small pieces of clay can be added to the clay you're working with. The lumpy slip can be left on a brick for a day, and then mixed with the throwing clay. If the clay used for throwing was hard, it can be added to the lumpy slip when the job is done.

▶ **3.** When turning, keep the clay organized as you work. Clay cut from the lump can be left on a brick to keep it separate from the clay that will be turned. When you have finished, mix it with the clay from the chuck; if it's gotten too dry, poke several holes into it with the needle tool, add a little water, and cover it. Partly dried turning clay should be kept separate and left to dry out completely for recycling. When you have accumulated a certain amount, reuse it. Clay is always recycled and should never be thrown away.

alternate them. Then cover it so that the next time it will be easier to wedge and will be homogeneous.

It's just as important to store the clay correctly after working with it as it is to keep it in good condition while working with it.

The type of clay you use will depend on the type of piece you're making on the wheel.

◀ **1.** Sometimes, wedging moist clay on the table and moving it from one end to another can harden it, since wood absorbs excess water from the clay.

◀ **3.** Leave the clay on a table for several hours or an entire day. When you'll be able to use the clay depends on the ambient temperature and the thickness of the coils. Clay should not be wedged on a plaster surface as a way of absorbing any excess moisture. Plaster spoils clay, causing it to lose its plasticity and to crack easily.

◀ **2.** If, despite everything, the clay is still too sticky and cannot be properly wedged, you can make it into rings or coils.

▼ **4.** If the clay is lumpy, wedge it more thoroughly. Press down with the palm of your hand in a forward and downward direction to work the clay. In this way, any lumps or hard pieces can easily be found and removed.

Recycling clay that's totally dried out

When you have a large amount of dry or partly dried clay, you will need to restore it.

To make this job as simple as possible, the clay should be completely dry; if it isn't, put it on a piece of newspaper or sheet of plastic on the floor to keep it clean and let it dry out. Drying it in the sun speeds up the process. Freshly recuperated clay should be left for at least a month, but three or four months is even better. If you need to keep clay for a long time, it's best to do so when it's a little more moist than usual. When clay rests for a certain time it rots and becomes more plastic. Mold spots don't harm the clay; on the contrary, they give it greater plasticity.

▲ **1.** Place the clay in a container, filling it no more than three-quarters full.

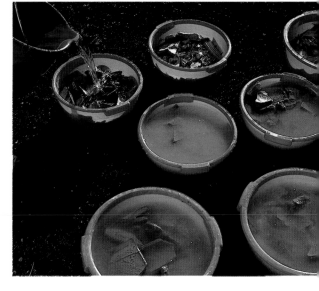

▲ **2.** Fill the container to cover all the clay in an inch of water and set aside for a day, or for at least four hours.

▼ **4.** Place bricks on a flat surface to form a square.

▼ **3.** The next day, stir with a stick and leave again. Without moving it, remove the excess water. If it was not completely dry when you recovered it, put it through the mixer; otherwise it will be lumpy after it's restored. A propeller-shaped mixer on an electric drill will work. If recuperated clay can be kept for some time, the lumps tend to disappear.

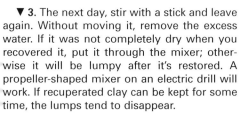

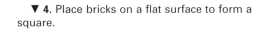

▶ **5.** Place a cloth (not cotton, which rots with moisture) and pour the clay into the square.

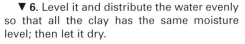

▼ **6.** Level it and distribute the water evenly so that all the clay has the same moisture level; then let it dry.

▶ **7.** After a few days, when the clay begins to crack, score it with a stick to form a grid pattern. That way the clay does not split apart, and it continues to dry out.

▶ **8.** The final drying stage can be accelerated by placing the small bricks on their side.

Throwing errors: How to avoid them

A study of various pieces during throwing and turning, together with several examples of the most common problems and how to solve them, will help the ceramist learn to throw correctly.

It's difficult to make any progress without first mastering the basic pieces. These basic forms are considered to be the bowl, the cylinder and the vase. It's a good idea to cut open the pieces until you make them correctly.

Typical errors in throwing

To make progress on the potter's wheel, you have to be able to recognize errors and their causes. Any imperfections can be seen by slicing the pieces in half after they're finished. At the outset, all pieces have some irregularities, but these flaws accumulate as the work goes on. This is the time to learn what they are so you can cure them.

▶ Hold the nylon or metal wire taut by each end and slice the piece energetically. Remove one half without touching the other so you don't damage it, and study it. It's important you cut through cleanly and evenly to obtain a cross section worth studying.

The bowl

The size of the inside of a bowl's base must be proportionate to the outside; that is, if the interior diameter is small, the outside diameter must follow suit; otherwise the base will contain too much clay.

The inside base of the bowl should be curved. The center should be the lowest part, and the surface should be mostly even.

The lower part of the walls should be a little thicker. If this is not the case, it's difficult to create large pieces, since they cave in.

No part of the wall should be thinner than the edge of the mouth. This upper edge should also be parallel to the base. You should understand how a bowl is constructed so it has sufficient strength and will not collapse.

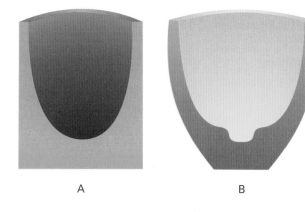

A   B

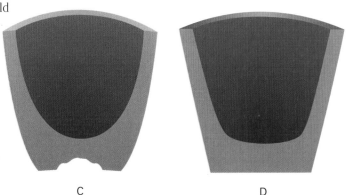

C   D

A. The internal shape should correspond to the exterior, or else the pieces will be too bulky. See step 8, page 69.

B. The internal base should be curved and be mostly smooth at every point. See step 8, page 69.

C. The outside of base of the bowl should be flat. Any holes mean that you applied too little pressure to the upper part of the lump before opening it up. Cracks may also appear. See step 2, page 68.

D. If the lower interior wall forms an angle, this means you applied too much pressure on the clay in this area. You can correct this fault by applying more pressure on the inside center of the base.

E. There's too much water inside the piece. Before taking the piece off the wheel, remove the water with a sponge. (See "The right amount of moisture for throwing," pages 32 to 34). If the water is not removed, it can cause cracking.

F. This piece lacks a base. It's advisable to review "Working off the hump," pages 38 and 39.

G. The clay for the lump you have worked with was not properly chosen and the base contains too much clay. Review step 1, page 39.

H. This bowl is low and wide. Its shape is half bowl, half plate. You'll have to learn to make them taller and narrower at the base. See steps 1, 2, 3, and 4, page 70.

E

F

G

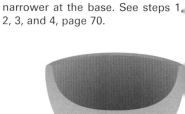

H

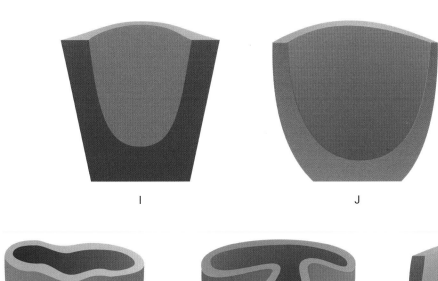

I

J

I. This piece is too thick; you should thin it out and use the clay to make a larger piece.

J. A lopsided piece. The left side is thicker than the right. You should review the chapter "Centering the clay," pages 35 to 43.

K. A piece with a badly cut rim. Review "Cutting rims with the needle tool," page 54.

L. A wrinkled piece. This happens when you take too long and the clay has been handled too much. It can also happen when there's too much water or the clay is very soft. It's a good idea to work with fresh clay that's stronger, and to pay attention to the amount of water you use.

M. No part of the walls should be thinner than the top. With a large piece, this could cause a cave-in. Review the exercise "The bowl," pages 68 and 69.

K

L

M

The cylinder

The inside base of the cylinder is flat and the walls are perpendicular to the base. The section of the wall adjacent to the base is slightly thicker than the upper part. With a small piece, this difference is not noticeable; with a large piece it's more evident. It all depends on the type of clay you're using. If the walls are very thick, you should modify the piece because that's a defect.

It's important to know how to make cylinders correctly, since many pieces are based on this shape. Defects can be clearly seen when these vessels measure between ten and twelve inches, since at this point the hands are working separately and with quite a lot of clay.

These structures should be made in under thirty minutes during the learning stage. After this time the clay sinks instead of rising. It is also important to know the type and hardness of the material, because if the clay is too soft it's difficult to make thin walls.

A

B

C

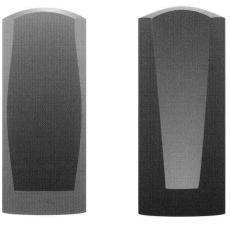

D

E

A. There's too much clay in the lower part of the piece and this alters the shape of the cylinder; the clay at the lower part should be pressed more firmly so that the inside and outside have the same shape. See step 3, page 40, and step 4, page 41.

B. The lower inside wall of this cylinder is too thick, and it has an abrupt shoulder halfway up the piece. This is a typical mistake, and it can't be corrected until you master this structure. Review how to apply pressure to the clay (see step 10, page 83).

C. There's too much water inside the piece. Control the water more carefully; if that doesn't work, turn with slip. Excess water causes the base of pieces to crack.

D. This error is more typical of bowls than of cylinders. If this happens, the wall will bend at this point. These cylinders usually don't remain straight, so you can cut them open, and they collapse when you're working on them.

E. The base has not been opened up correctly. The internal circumference is small in proportion to the exterior, meaning that there's too much clay in the walls of the base. More pressure should be applied to create a larger piece. Review steps 9 and 10, page 42.

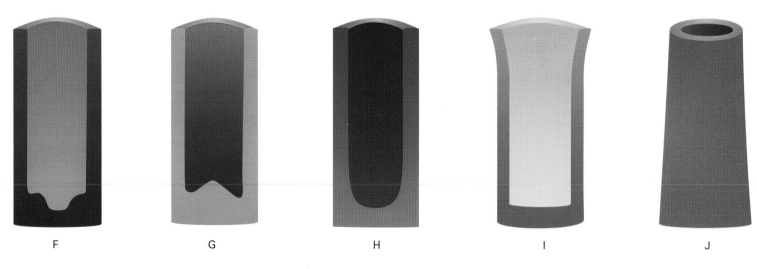

F   G   H   I   J

F. The inside of the base was not made flat. If a drop of water is put inside, it should be able to settle on any part of the base, and not just in the center. Review steps 3 and 4, page 39.

G. The inside of the base has a hump in the center. The base should be worked more thoroughly with the fingertips. See step 2, page 40.

H. The angles of the base are rounded. Clay has accumulated here and the resulting piece will be quite heavy. Review how to work on the edge of the base with the bent index finger of your left hand. See steps 3 and 4, page 39.

I. It is common when throwing to work out of perpendicular to the wheel head, making the pieces more conical than cylindrical, with a wider mouth. Keep an eye on the profile of the piece as you work.

J. Wider at the base than the top. This happens because of the difficulty of seeing if the clay is correctly distributed while you work. It's a good idea to throw cylinders to spot any flaws and learn how to guide the clay with your hands. Check the profile of the piece as you work.

The vase

The vase is based on the structure of the cylinder. To build a vase correctly, the clay must be distributed properly when you make the cylinder.

The lower walls of a vase must be like those of a bowl for the piece to remain upright, unless you are working with very strong clay. This means that the lower wall of the piece should be slightly thicker where it touches the base, and at no point on the wall should it be thinner than the rim.

If you haven't made the cylinder properly before making a vase, the vase generally ends up with too much clay in the base. It is important to control the amount of water used in throwing and to avoid using sticks with sponges on the end to remove excess water. This defect will interfere with your progress on the wheel.

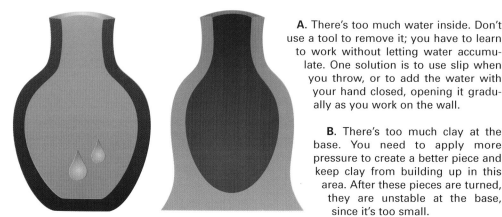

A   B

A. There's too much water inside. Don't use a tool to remove it; you have to learn to work without letting water accumulate. One solution is to use slip when you throw, or to add the water with your hand closed, opening it gradually as you work on the wall.

B. There's too much clay at the base. You need to apply more pressure to create a better piece and keep clay from building up in this area. After these pieces are turned, they are unstable at the base, since it's too small.

C. The base of the vase hasn't been opened up enough; this means that the cylinder was not made properly. When these pieces are lightened, about twenty or thirty percent of the clay is removed. They should be turned when the clay is not too dry; when removing the upper layer, which is the driest, great care must be taken so that the piece retains its shape.

D. The rim is cut crooked; when the vase is done, it's important to cut the rim parallel to the base. When turning, the piece should be centered by the rim.

E. This piece has a section along the wall that's thinner than the top. This fault occurs easily when throwing a ball-shaped lump. These volumes may collapse while they're being thrown.

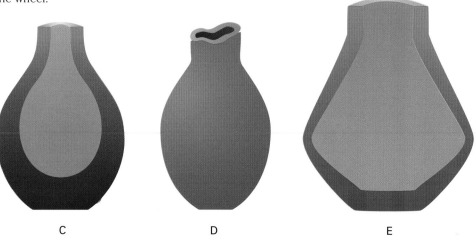

C   D   E

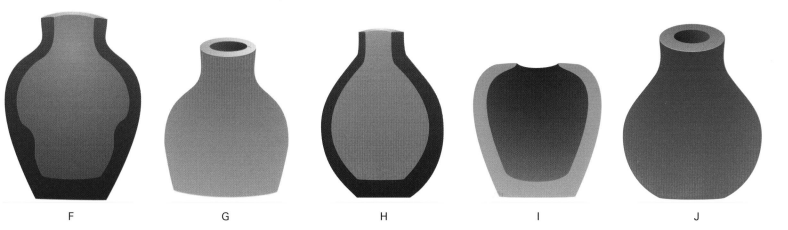

F   G   H   I   J

F. There is a bulge in the middle of the inside wall. This can easily occur if the vase is shaped several times and you fail to detect any resulting irregularities.

G. This vase was made from a cylinder that was too wide in relation to its height. That makes it too squat. If that's done on purpose, it's not a flaw, but it's more common when you don't have much experience. This piece should be made from a narrower cylinder.

H. This vase was thrown off center and has one wall thicker than the other. It's a good idea to check the centering.

I. Too little clay was used to build this piece, and it has no neck. Review how to make closed shapes, and avoid opening the neck of the piece too much when you work so you'll have enough material to make the neck.

J. If the edge is this thick when you cut the mouth, the piece should be thinned down. Utilitarian pieces should be thin.

Typical flaws in turning

After you've eliminated errors in throwing, you have to deal with turning. We can differentiate these types of defects: ones produced by handling the clay when it's too soft or too dry; and ones that result from lack of experience in turning.

There are defects that are common to all three basic pieces, and others that are characteristics of each. There are still others that arise when you use methods different from those explained in this book, but we couldn't cover every eventuality in this manual.

The bowl

Bowls have to be completely centered for turning. If you have trouble getting the rim parallel to the wheel head, you should modify the chuck so it is easier to center the pieces.

A. It can happen that a piece that was correctly thrown is turned off center. If this happens, the mouth will be thicker on one side than the other. To conceal the defect, see step 13, page 64.

B. Pieces that are turned when the clay is too dry frequently break at the rim. Clay is stronger when it's leather hard, rather than entirely dry.

C. Small cracks can be seen around the mouth of the piece; this is another typical defect of turning objects when they are too dry.

D. If the base is not flattened during the turning, when the rim is made parallel to the wheel head the piece is turned off center, and one side comes out higher than the other. See page 71, step 3.

▶ If you can't spot the defects in the pieces you have made, we recommend centering them on a banding wheel and observing the piece while you rotate it by hand to see if the piece is not straight, has a warped rim, or has one side different from the other. When rotating the wheel head, you can easily spot any problem the piece may have by studying the profile and the rim.

A   B   C   D

Cylinders

Cylinders must be thrown correctly, but since this is seldom the case with the first ones you make, you should lighten them by turning, even if that makes them conical. The next time you throw, your hands will be more sensitive to different thicknesses.

A. If you turn a cylinder with a crooked rim and don't use the same reference point when centering it, then each side may be different in profile, that is, asymmetrical. To avoid this, you have to cut the rim correctly when you throw, and if that doesn't work, you have to do so when you turn the piece. See page 63, steps 5 through 8.

B. You should not turn a piece with a warped rim; otherwise it may open up and lose its shape.

C. Another typical defect that occurs in turning is for the inside edge of the piece to become deformed, resembling a cone. You have to control the shape of the piece while you work.

D. If the piece is turned when it's too dry, it may break at the rim. This defect is more characteristic of cylinders than of bowls.

E. To fashion a raised lip the two concentric circles at the base of the cylinder must be made at the same time. If the piece comes off center between the two levels, the lip may turn out wider on one side than the other.

A

B

C

D

E

Vases

Necks are the most difficult part to turn to achieve an aesthetic effect. Flexible ribs can help us solve many of these problems. Time is never wasted when turning; on the contrary, it contributes to mastery of the wheel.

A. A certain area may sink in during turning. If this happens, stop turning, raise the dent to the level of the wall, and let the piece dry a little more. If the piece has a wide mouth, this is an easy repair. If it's narrow, even it out it by blowing into the vessel. When the piece is drier, you can continue turning.

B. This piece is unstable. It was thrown with a lot of clay at the base which was removed by turning. Review the section on making cylinders and pressing the clay outward at the base (see step 10, page 83).

C. This piece was turned with the neck off center. Pieces that are turned without centering at the neck often turn out asymmetrical. Vases must be centered at the rim for turning.

D. The base is not parallel to the rim; this means that the piece is higher on one side than on the other.

E. This vase was turned with a tool that scored the surface. Scratches can be eliminated with flexible ribs used on the wall of the piece.

F. The rim is badly cut. If the mouth appears warped, cut it before you start turning.

A

B

C

D

E

F

How to correct defects by turning

The number of problems you encounter will depend on how you turn the pieces on the wheel head. If they are thrown well and handled when the clay has the right hardness, they will be easier to turn. Below we analyze the most common problems and how to solve them.

► **1.** This piece has a hole and a small crack in the base.

► **2.** If the clay is dry, score the base with the needle and add some slip to soften it.

◄ **3.** Then add some clay, pressing down hard to fill the hole. If the clay is soft, skip step 2.

► **4.** The same method is used for pieces that were thrown directly on the wheel head and lack clay in a certain spot. Once you have added the clay, cover the piece and continue turning the following day. That way the entire base is uniformly hard, and that keeps the tool from digging into it.

► **5.** When turning, you may have to fix a crooked rim. If so, it will have to be cut off. If the clay is too hard to use the needle, you can use a utility knife. Use one with a thin blade that's free of rust. Dentist's tools are ideal for this. Center the piece and insert the knife into the mouth.

◄ **6.** When the blade goes all the way through, the resulting ring is lifted off. Don't use a knife with a blade longer than $1/2$ inch; otherwise it will bend while you work.

▼ **8.** And lastly, the inside edge.

► **7.** Once the edge is removed, bevel the outside edge.

▶ **9.** If the edge is too thick after it's been cut, thin it a little. This can be done with a piece of flexible rib, working perpendicular to the wall of the piece.

▶ **10.** If you encounter a major irregularity when you flatten the base . . .

▼ **11.** . . . stop the wheel and remove the bump with a flexible tool.

▲ **12.** Then flatten the base as usual. It's sometimes useful to work with a soft rib, and if that doesn't work, with a flexible angle tool.

◀ **14.** If a piece has been made with no foot, you can add one. Flatten the base, score it, and apply some slip.

▼ **15.** Add a coil, fit one end over the other, and cut off the excess.

▲ **13.** Once the piece has been turned, if the rim is off center, center it to disguise the defect. With your ring finger on the outside of the rim, place the small tool on the right-angle side and modify the edge of the rim by removing the area that's off center. Modify about an inch of the mouth and make the wall even. Be sure to keep your hands completely still while you work.

▼ **16.** Press the coil down onto the piece on the inside and the outside.

◀ **17.** The foot is thrown and cut with the needle.

◀ **18.** Remove the rough edges. Lift it off the wheel head, cover the entire piece with plastic for a day, and turn it the following day.

▼ **19.** Always watch the piece closely while turning to make sure it doesn't lose its shape. If a bowl is too soft when it's turned, the walls will become deformed.

▲ **20.** Chatter marks are one of the main problems beginners encounter in turning. Some tools (such as this one) produce lots of chatter marks. As soon as they appear, set the tool aside and let the piece dry out a little more.

▲ **21.** If you want to remove chatter marks without waiting for the piece to dry, a wire loop tool is ideal, since it doesn't cut, and it allows you to work on the clay while it's still soft.

▶ **22.** Another way to remove chatter marks once the clay has dried out some more is to hold the flexible tool in this position, perpendicular to the dents.

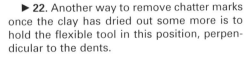

▼ **23.** Change the angle as you work, as shown here, and hold the tool at a right angle to the dents to remove them. The problem stems from the moistness of the clay with respect to the tool you're using. However, some tools are just difficult to use.

▶ **24.** Use the sponge only when the piece is finished and it's easy to see the entire form. Squeeze out the sponge to avoid cracking the pieces with excess water. This is an excellent finish for any subsequent glaze to adhere to. If you use the sponge too much and the clay contains sand, the sand will rise to the surface.

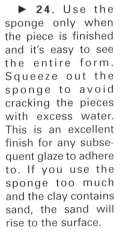

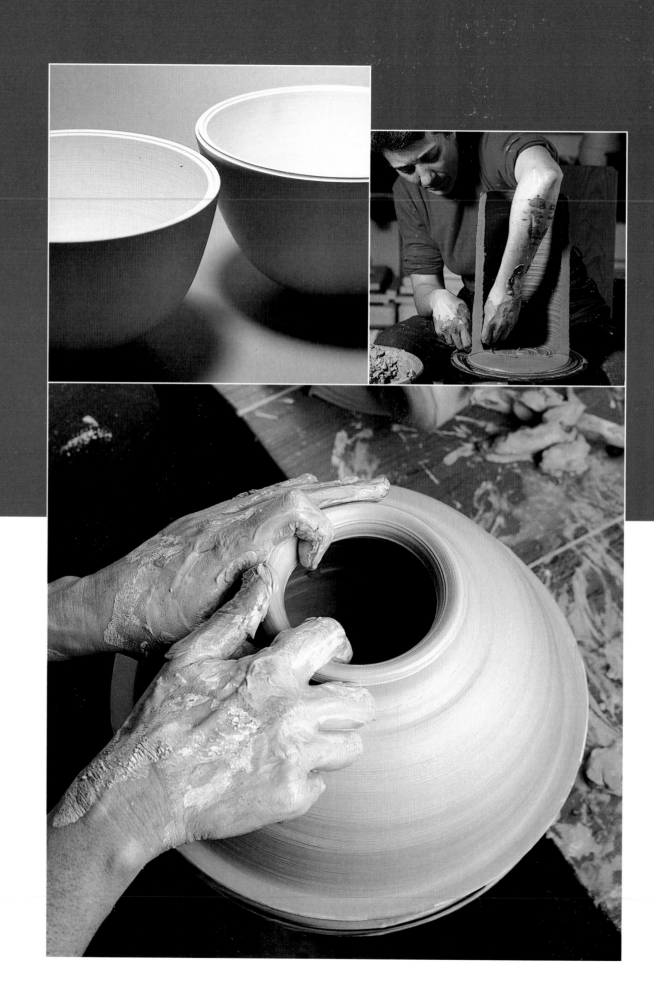

Step-by-step

*T*he "Step-by-step" sections present every phase of each process. In most books, you have to imagine what happens between one sequence and another. That's why in this chapter we attempt to describe clearly and precisely how to carry out a series of basic procedures on the wheel, so that you can achieve specific results without having to rely too much on your imagination. This means that the procedures are amply illustrated and accompanied by texts that may seem a bit repetitive; but they'll come in handy when you're battling clay on the wheel and trying to achieve a certain result.

Bowls

The bowl is considered one of the basic pieces that can be made on the wheel. It forms the basis for countless pieces, so it's a good idea to be thoroughly familiar with it. What should a bowl be like? The inside should be rounded. The central point will be the deepest part. If a drop of water is put into the bowl, it should slide down the sides and come to rest in the center. This characteristic is appreciated in the culinary and chemical fields, among others. If you were to cut a bowl in half, the cross section would show the lower part of the wall to be somewhat thicker than the upper; no point along the piece should be thinner than the upper part. If these two rules are not observed, large pieces can't be made because they will collapse.

▲ We can separate bowls into two types: one that uses a narrow base and a high wall, and the other with a wide base and a low wall.

▲ If the bowl is to be used for drinking tea or coffee, you should decide if you want the liquid to keep warm for a long time or to cool off quickly. If the liquid is to be kept warm for a while, the wall should be straight, or it should curve in slightly at the rim.

▲ Otherwise, the rim of the bowl should curve slightly outward.

▼ **3.** Insert your thumb into the top.

▲ **1.** Make a narrow, high cone.

▶ **2.** Forcefully compress the top part before opening it up.

► **4.** Open the cone outward by pressing with your index fingers on the inside of the rim. Your other fingers should be placed on the outside about an inch and a half below the rim.

◄ **5.** Select the part of the clay that will actually become the bowl.

► **6.** Pull the clay up using your left thumb and index finger and your right index and middle fingers. The thumbs should stay together.

▼ **7.** Thin the walls by applying pressure. If you pull your hands toward you, the rim of the piece opens up more; as you move them upward, the mouth closes in.

▼ **8.** If you want the inside of the piece to be wider, make the base wider; don't forget that the center is the lowest part. Even when all the fingers of the left hand are inside the piece, press only with either your middle or index finger. At the same time, apply pressure on the base with your right hand to regulate the thickness.

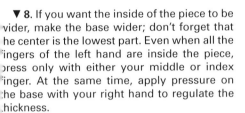

◄ **9.** Cut the rim with a needle tool (see "Cutting rims with a needle tool," p. 54).

▼ **10.** Smooth off the rim to remove any rough edges left from cutting.

▼ **11.** Cut the base (see "Cutting a piece off the hump," p. 54).

How to perfect the shape of a bowl

If the inside of the base was widened too much in step 8 on page 69, you can modify the piece so that the base is smaller and the wall more vertical. It's a good idea to practice this on small pieces, which are easier to work on. You should cut the first pieces you make in half so you can find the flaws and correct them (see "Throwing errors: How to avoid them," pages 58–65).

◀ **1.** Cup your hands around the piece and apply inward pressure. This should be done gently, without applying too much force, and slowly, to prevent the clay from bending.

▲ **2.** Pull the rim upward and inward without applying pressure, beginning with the middle of the piece and moving upward.

◀ **3.** The same position as in step 2 from the worker's viewpoint.

◀ **4.** Repeat the operation beginning with the lower part. You can see how the shape of the bowl has changed.

▶ **5.** Pull the clay upward by pressing it with your right index finger and your left middle finger. You can also use both index fingers. The thumbs work in unison.

▼ **6.** Cut the rim.

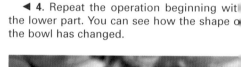

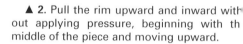

▲ **7.** Smooth the rough edges and cut the piece at the base.

◀ **8.** If you want the bowl to open more, press outward with your right hand while your left hand controls the opening.

Turning the outside of the bowl

First, you should turn the exterior of the bowl. The bowl should have the desired weight and shape when you're done working on the outside, since this is when it is most moist. Don't make the foot on the base until you've brought the piece to its final dimensions.

▶ **1.** Check to see if the rim of the piece is solid enough. If it keeps its shape when you pick it up by the rim, it's ready for turning. Otherwise, it should be left to dry some more.

▶ **2.** Make a chuck and check to see that it fits the piece. Use a heat gun to dry the area of the chuck that will contact the bowl.

▼ **4.** Center the bowl again and flatten the base with a flexible rectangular metal rib held firmly in your hand.

◀ **3.** Check the thickness of the piece by feeling it with your fingers.

Slide it over the chuck and center it. Place your ring fingers or middle fingers under the rim. Lift the piece a half-inch and lower it, letting it slide over your thumbs. Repeat the operation until the mouth of the piece is parallel to the base of the chuck.

Start the wheel without the piece on it to make sure the area of the chuck that will hold the piece is correctly centered. If so, you can begin turning. Otherwise, modify the chuck.

▼ **5.** Place the corner of the rib at the center of the bowl. Keep both hands together as you hold the rib in your right hand and brace it against your left index finger.

◀ **6.** Scrape excess clay off of the base and the walls with a looped tool. If the walls are too thick, thin them out; if they are thin, the shape will be right. If this tool doesn't remove the clay because it has dried too much, find one that cuts better.

◄ **7.** Smooth and shape the bowl with a flexible rib held perpendicular to it to remove any irregularities.

► **8.** Finish smoothing off the sides, this time with the rib held parallel to the walls to remove any ridges you may have created in the previous steps.

▼ **9.** Trace a circle with a small trimming tool inside the foot of the base. Rest the tool against your left thumb to keep it stable during the process.

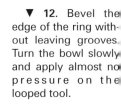

◄ **10.** Carve out the inside from the center to the edge, while protecting the foot with your thumb so that the tool doesn't damage it.

▼ **11.** Flatten the inside of the foot ring with a small piece of flexible rib.

▼ **12.** Bevel the edge of the ring without leaving grooves. Turn the bowl slowly and apply almost no pressure on the looped tool.

◄ **14**. Before removing the piece, dry your hands well on a towel. Pick the piece up by the rim and place it onto a clean bat.

▼ **16**. Then make the outer circle, parallel to the first one and about 1¹/₂ inches away.

▲ **13**. With a well wrung-out sponge, go over the surface of the piece to keep it from becoming too glossy, and so that the glaze will adhere properly later on.

► **15**. If you want the base to have a raised rim, make two concentric circles without moving the piece. First make the inner circle.

▼ **17**. Lower the area around the outer circle to modify the shape of the piece. Use the rib to straighten the profile once again, since there may be a hump.

► **18**. Once the piece is finished, go over it with a wrung-out sponge, stop the wheel, remove the piece by lifting it at the rim, and place it on a clean bat.

When you make this type of base, a bump is left on the lower part of the bowl. Follow steps 7 and 8 on page 72 to remove it.

If you make the base rim before you take the piece to its final dimensions, you must make sure the walls are the right thickness once you have finished with the rim.

73

Turning the inside of the bowl

Most pieces are not turned on the inside, except for bowls and a couple of other pieces. If the bowl was thrown correctly, the inside will simply need to be smoothed off. But if it was deformed during turning or the base was not thrown properly, this is the time to correct the defects. Once the pieces are finished, review the problems you had during the turning process.

► **1.** Open up the chuck (see "Turning with chucks," pages 46–53). Trim the inside edge, and use the heat gun to dry only the area where the bowl will touch it, not the entire chuck.

▲ **2.** Center the bowl and smooth off the inner walls with a small flexible rib.

▲ **3.** Bevel the outside edge of the rim with a looped tool.

▲ **4.** Bevel the inside edge.

▲ **5.** Go over the interior with a wrung-out damp sponge.

▲ **6.** Stop the wheel and wipe your hands on a towel. Grasp the piece near the rim, remove it from the chuck and place it on a clean bat.

► **7.** A variety of bowl shapes.

How to make a bowl on a bat

When you make a larger bowl, the mouth may be too large to remove from the wheel without deforming it. In this case, it should be thrown on a support.

It's a good idea to work the piece well so that the clay is evenly distributed, keeping the mouth more closed and not opening it all the way until the end. This bowl is a little more difficult than the previous one because your hands work independently.

▲ **1.** Prepare the base and place the bat onto it (see "Bats," pages 44–45). Place some clay onto the plaster bat and center it.

▲ **2.** Open up a hole in the center, first with your right index finger, then with all the fingers of both hands. Press the clay from the center to within an inch and a half of the base.

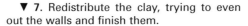

▲ **5.** Bend the rim slightly inward. The hands can't work together because the mouth is too wide.

▲ **3.** Work on the base so that the deepest point is in the center and it's a little less than an inch thick.

▼ **6.** Press the base again with your hands apart. Make a fist and hook your index fingers around your thumbs. The base must be finished first, since it will be more difficult later on.

▲ **4.** Press the clay starting at the base in order to eliminate unnecessary thickness and distribute it throughout the walls.

▼ **7.** Redistribute the clay, trying to even out the walls and finish them.

▼ **8.** Once the walls have the right thickness, give the bowl its final shape. Starting with your left hand in the center of the base and your right hand on the outside, move them along the walls. If you want to open up the mouth, apply more pressure toward the outside with your left hand. If you want to keep it the same, press both hands toward the top.

▲ **9.** Once the piece is finished, run a wooden tool along the base to make sure it comes off the wheel cleanly. Allow it to dry longer than pieces that will be turned, since this one will be turned only at the base.

▲ **10.** Put the clay on the wheel to make a chuck. Make a hole down to the wheel head. The rim should be thickest. Cut off the outside edge of the rim with a needle tool.

▲ **11.** Next cut off some more from the resulting rim to be sure that the outside circumference is completely centered. Then cut off the top (see "Turning with chucks," pages 46–53).

▶ **12.** Use the electric heat gun to dry the part of the chuck that will support the piece.

▶ **13.** Flatten the base of the piece and trim down the lower part. This piece won't be turned inside or outside, and you can leave the marks from your fingers on it.

▲ **14.** Make the foot ring. First trace a circle with a small scraper; then remove clay from the center with a wire loop tool, since this is a large base.

▶ **15.** Go over the base with a sponge and place the piece on a clean bat to dry. Some ceramists use the technique of turning only the base of the piece.

► This base has a raised ring, as if a small cylinder were placed on top of the bowl.

▲ The ring on this piece is not free-standing; rather, it's a continuation of the shape of the bowl.

◄ The rims of these bowls were cut at a slant. They are more fragile, but highly decorative from an artistic viewpoint.

▼ Some ridges were added here with a small loop tool during turning.

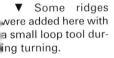

▼ The turning was done in such a way that the rims were not left so sharp that they could break easily. In the photo you can see that one of them is chipped.

Cylinders

A cylindrical shape is totally different from a bowl. The inside base must be flat and the walls perpendicular to the base. A drop of water placed into a cylinder can come to rest at any point on the base.

This major difference in the internal structures of the bowl and the cylinder is fundamental to throwing.

You need to master both of these pieces first before moving on. They are very different, but once you have mastered them, you will see that other pieces are nothing more than minor variations on these two.

How to throw a cylinder

If you want to make a small cylinder and the type of clay allows it, you can throw it off the hump. A larger cylinder should be made directly on the wheel.

This piece is intentionally done directly on the wheel, since the process involves one of the most difficult tasks for the beginner: centering the clay that contacts the wheel.

▲ If you're working with a clay that has high porcelain content, the lower part of the wall can be a fraction of an inch thicker than the upper. If you cut some recently finished pieces in two, they may become slightly deformed like the one shown here. It all depends on the quality of the material you're working with.

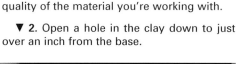

▼ **2.** Open a hole in the clay down to just over an inch from the base.

▲ **1.** Place a lump of clay on the wheel and center it. Make sure the part that touches the wheel is centered as well; this is the most difficult part.

◄ **3.** Use the tips of your fingers to flatten the base as much as possible. As you work on the base, thin it to about ³/₄ inch.

▼ **4.** Press on the clay of the inside wall at the base with your right index and middle fingers. Both hands are joined at the thumbs.

▲ **5.** With your right thumbnail, cut away the bottom edge of clay at the base, since all the clay will have to be pressed from the outside.

◄ 6. Squeeze on the base to pull the clay upward.

▼ 9. Cut the rim parallel to the wheel head. Then cut the base. Dry your hands, remove the piece from the wheel head, and place it onto a clean bat.

◄ 7. Try to work perpendicular to the wheel, so that the piece is cylindrical, with the rim slightly narrower than the base.

▼ 8. Smooth the piece off with a rib. The hand inside applies outward pressure. If the piece was not made correctly and you press inward with the tool to alter the shape, the rib can easily dig into the wall and leave marks.

► 10. The piece should not be turned to a cone shape. This is one of the most common problems that beginners need to avoid.

▼ 11. Should this occur, remove the excess clay at the bottom with your thumb as before.

▲ 12. Again press the clay at the base and pull the clay up perpendicular to the wheel head. This increases the size of the cylinder. While you work, watch the profile of the piece; if it starts to become conical again, apply more outward pressure with your left hand to keep the shape cylindrical.

Turning a cylinder

When you turn a cylinder, start with the outside and finish with the rim. Like most pieces, cylinders are not turned on the inside. The lines that remain in the clay are a sign that it was made on a wheel. Normally only very open pieces such as bowls are turned on the inside.

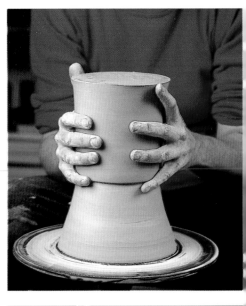

▶ **1.** Make a chuck, dry it with a heat gun, and put the piece on it face down. Turn on the wheel, then remove the piece and make sure that the chuck is centered. Remove the mark left on the chuck and dry it with the heat gun only where the mark was left. Center it again.

▶ **2.** Center the piece by holding it in both hands with your little fingers under the rim. If the chuck is right, you can go and wash your hands. Otherwise, modify it.

▲ **3.** Smooth off the base to make it parallel to the rim. Then thin the walls with the trimming tool until the piece has the right weight.

▲ **4.** Smooth off the wall with a flexible rib held perpendicular to it.

▲ **5.** Don't work on the ends of this shape because you won't be able to keep the piece totally cylindrical.

◀ **6.** If the piece becomes deformed when you remove it from the chuck, fix it by running your index finger along the wall from top to bottom. Don't place the piece on the chuck if the chuck is misshapen.

◀ **7.** Only when the piece has attained a weight appropriate to its size should you make the foot ring. With the small trimming tool, trace a line parallel to the outer edge of the base at a distance of an inch and a half. Use your left thumb to protect the rim.

▲ **8.** Hollow out the center of the rim with a trimming tool. Then go over the piece with a lightly damp sponge.

▲ **9.** If you want a raised ring, make two concentric lines at the same time without disturbing the piece.

▲ **10.** Hollow out the middle.

▲ **11.** Hollow out the outside.

◄ **12.** If you wish, go over it with the flexible rib to make a right angle.

▼ **14.** When the piece has dried for a few hours, make another chuck and place the piece face up in it, centering it at the mouth. Turn it with a wire loop tool to bevel the inside and outside edges. Go over the rim with a sponge.

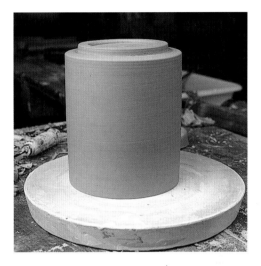

▲ **13.** Wipe your hands well with a towel. Remove the piece from the chuck and place it on a clean bat to dry.

▼ **15.** Allow to dry completely on a clean bat. The piece is now finished.

Cylindrical forms

The cylinder is the shape on which a great number of thrown pieces are based. You should practice making large and small cylinders, following the different centering and opening techniques (see "Centering the clay," pages 35–43). Don't take longer than thirty minutes to make these pieces, since after that time, the pieces have a tendency to compact rather than being pulled upward.

▲ **1.** How you center the clay will depend on the size of the piece to be thrown. If the piece is to be large and tall, the lump of clay being centered should center high. Once it's centered, open it up, first with one thumb and then with the other. Add a handful of lump-free slip to it, and then push your clenched fist into the clay to within an inch and a half of the wheel.

▲ **2.** Work the base with your fingertips and your fist.

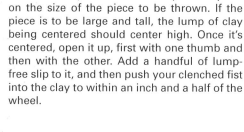

◄ **3.** Squeeze the clay in the base to pull the clay upward.

▲ **6.** If the piece is too wide at the base reduce it. If you want to throw properly, you must master this exercise. First reduce the neck by applying inward pressure with both hands

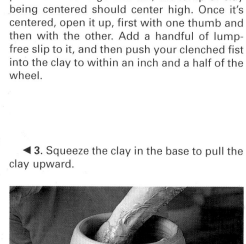

▲ **4.** Move your hands upward along the piece to distribute the clay.

▲ **5.** Repeat the operation as often as necessary until the walls are even.

▶ **7.** Then wet the outside of the piece with your hands, running them up and down over the piece. The water will soak into the piece and produce slip.

▶ **8.** Place your hands at the base as if you were centering it, and move them upward to reduce the diameter of the piece.

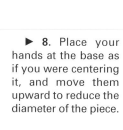

▲ 9. When you reduce the diameter, the piece becomes conical, with thick bunches of clay. Repeat the process of pulling the clay up from the base to the rim to thin it and make the walls perpendicular to the wheel.

▶ 11. With the hands staggered, the hands begin together, but the one on the outside remains lower.

▼ 13. When the piece is done, cut the rim parallel to the base. If you want a smooth surface, go over it with a tool. Allow to dry, and if you wish, turn the base.

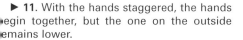

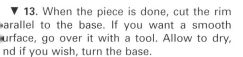

◀ 10. The clay can be pulled up in two ways: with the hands parallel, the outside hand first moves up to the level of the one on the inside.

▲ 12. The piece should have a cylindrical rather than a conical shape so you can control the thickness of the base and the walls. All the clay on the wheel should be incorporated into the piece, and the walls must be thin. While working, keep an eye on the profile of the piece to control its shape.

▲ 14. Another way to pull the clay up is to apply pressure with a rib. Some ceramists use this method.

▶ 15. A piece turned only at the base.

Vases

*T*here are two ways to throw vases. One is to shape the piece from the base up, as if it were growing. The other is to throw a cylinder shape, neck it, and shape the vase from there. Both systems work for making a vase, but the first method is more difficult for the beginner, since it's hard to know how big a piece you can make with the clay you have. So if you haven't mastered the process, you may not have enough clay to finish a vase if you make it that way. With the second process there's always enough clay to finish the piece, and you may even have clay left over. This is the way potters do it. To master this technique, it's a good idea to begin by making pieces with necks as wide as your hand so you can put it inside as you turn and judge the thickness of the walls. Once you have mastered this step, you can progress to collaring and producing completely concentric vessels.

How to make a wide-necked vase

To achieve good results in throwing rounded vases, you must finish the base in one or two steps and not touch it again. After this, the piece is worked as little as possible. If the base is worked too much and the criteria for bowls are not observed, the piece will collapse.

◄ What's a vase shape like? The lower part should be slightly thicker than the upper, as with a bowl. For the piece to support itself, no point along the wall can be thinner than the top. Also, the base should not be unnecessarily thick, and the shape of the inner wall must follow that of the outer wall. It's a good idea to cut open your first pieces to see if the clay is correctly distributed.

▲ **1.** Center the clay and open a hole.

▲ **2.** Work the base with your fingertips, o hold your hand as shown in the photo an turn your wrist. You can apply more force wit your knuckles than with your fingertips.

▼ **3.** Reduce the base by pressing upward from the base with the sides of your hands. Don't reduce the base if the walls are not uniform, because the piece could collapse.

▼ **4.** Use your thumb to remove excess clay that has accumulated at the base.

▼ **5.** Squeeze at the base and pull the cla up perpendicular to the wheel head. Don bring it up into a cone shape. Insert your han in the same position as your right hand in ste 2. Make the walls slightly thicker than yo would for a cylinder.

◄ **6.** Draw in the neck. This position is fundamental to making a vase correctly. Place your index fingers over the rim. The remainder of your left hand works open around the piece and supports it, while the other fingers of your right hand are bent to make the indentation of the neck. Keep your thumbs locked on the outside of the rim. With your hands in this position, squeeze inward to make the neck narrower.

► **7.** This is the same position, as you will see it.

◄ **9.** As your hands move up the wall, keep an eye on the profile of the piece to monitor its shape. If the neck of a vase happens to open up, stop what you're doing and squeeze it back in. That way, there will be enough clay to neck the piece, and you will be able to make any shape. When you resume work, go back to the same place where you left off. Check the thickness of the walls and eliminate any irregularities.

▲ **8.** Working upward from the base, press with the left hand on the inside to make it bulge out. The outside hand must move a little in advance of the one inside as they go up, or they can be staggered as they move up simultaneously. As you shape the pitcher, apply pressure to thin the walls.

▼ **10.** Use your right hand to apply slight pressure toward the center to narrow the neck.

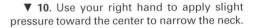

▼ **11.** Repeat the operation, this time with your left hand cupped inside the vase to make it curve out more.

▲ **12.** Continue to narrow the neck.

► **13.** Cut the rim parallel to the base.

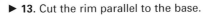

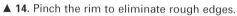

▲ **14.** Pinch the rim to eliminate rough edges.

▲ **15.** To smooth the walls, go over them with a reed smoothing tool. This is a tool used by ceramists in this instance.

▶ **16.** Cut the piece off, dry your hands, and remove it carefully from the wheel without digging in with your fingers. Place it on a clean bat.

How to make a narrow-necked vase

Once you have mastered making a wide-necked vase and have succeeded in making it light, you can move on to narrow-necked vases.

▶ **1.** Make a cylinder and collar it.

▶ **2.** Wet the outside of the piece.

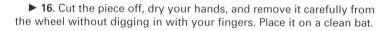

▼ **3.** Squeeze it starting at the base and pull the clay upward.

▼ **4.** Move your hands up.

▼ **5.** Press the clay in the base.

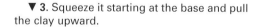

▲ **6.** Distribute the clay throughout the walls of the piece.

▲ **7.** Shape the piece, beginning with the base and finishing at the top.

▲ **8.** Draw in the neck to close the mouth some more. Only professionals shape vases in a single step. Until you master the technique, shape the vase in several steps.

▲ **9.** With your left middle and ring fingers on the inside and your right index finger on the outside, apply pressure to the neck to squeeze the clay upward.

◄ **10.** Reduce the neck by pressing inward with your middle fingers and your thumbs.

► **11.** As you squeeze from the outside to reduce the neck, it also becomes thicker and the clay builds up. Thin it the same way you did in step 9.

▼ **12.** Continue to thin the neck, squeezing on the outside with your fingertips.

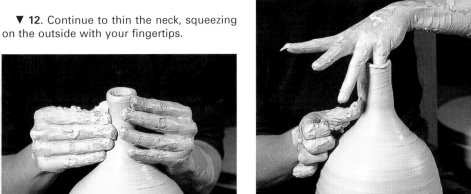

▲ **13.** Since the neck is very narrow, place your little finger inside. Squeeze with your thumb on the outside and your little finger on the inside.

► **14.** Go over the outside with a rib to remove the slip and touch up the shape of the piece.

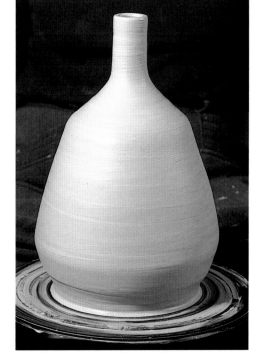

How to make a closed form

One challenge for beginners in throwing vases is making a closed form. Often, there's not enough clay left at the top to finish the piece. It's also very difficult to turn a closed form so that it remains centered. The following is a series of guidelines to help you avoid these problems and execute the tasks correctly.

► **1.** Make a cylinder that's slightly larger at the base than if you were making a tall, thin vase. Shape the piece from the base, pressing outward with your left hand and inward with your right hand.

▲ **2.** Squeeze in the neck.

▲ **3.** Press the clay of the walls in toward the neck so there will be enough clay to close it up. Don't leave uneven areas inside. Continue to squeeze in the neck and press on the walls again.

▲ **4.** Finish by closing the neck and breaking off the remaining stub. You should compress the clay well in this area once the stub has been removed to keep the closure from cracking as it dries.

▲ **5.** Go over the piece with a rib to remove slip.

▲ **6.** The shape of the closed form will differ according to where you apply the tool.

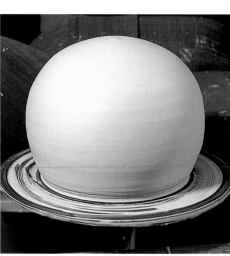

▼ **7.** Once the piece is done, remove it from the wheel with both hands and place it on a clean bat. If your hands are wet or the piece still has slip on it, it can easily slide out of your hands.

▼ **8.** After the piece has dried for twenty-four hours, make a hole in the base with a needle tool to let out the air that's trapped inside. If you don't make a hole, the piece will crack open at the top, which is the weakest part; as the piece dries, it shrinks, and the trapped air will cause it to crack.

Turning wide-necked vases

To make a well centered vase, you should start by turning the top. In order to use the same chuck to turn the entire vase, it's a good idea to reduce the diameter of the base a little before turning.

Don't work on the piece if the neck isn't perfectly centered. Before turning, check to see how moist the piece is and examine its weight and the thickness of the walls.

▼ **3.** Cut the top off with a long needle tool, and then bevel the outside and inside edges. Use the heat gun to dry only the area that will come into contact with the piece.

▲ **1.** Before you make the chuck, check to see if the piece has the right degree of moisture by pressing your thumb into the base to displace some clay. If it's easy to move, then the piece is too moist to turn. Once it has reached the appropriate degree of moisture, examine its structure.

◀ **2.** The chuck for turning the vase will be cylindrical, with walls nearly an inch thick, and open all the way down to the wheel. Use enough clay so that it keeps its shape when you turn the piece.

After the chuck is finished, make the upper rim thicker.

▲ **4.** Place the vase upside down on the chuck.

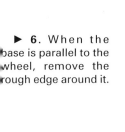

▶ **6.** When the base is parallel to the wheel, remove the rough edge around it.

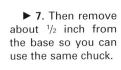

▲ **5.** Center the vase, holding it by the bottom with your hands opened wide.

▶ **7.** Then remove about ½ inch from the base so you can use the same chuck.

▼ **8.** Turn the piece over and center it, holding it by the neck.

▲ **10.** Once the piece has reached the right weight, go over it with a flexible rib to smooth it out. The best tool is the one that has one straight edge and one curved one. Work on the neck with the curved edge, and move it along the vertical wall from top to bottom and bottom to top. As you work, keep an eye on the profile of the piece. If the tool removes clay uniformly, you will see the results in the wall. If not, you will see an indentation in the profile. In that case, work with the tool until you level the wall.

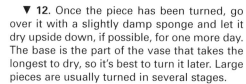

▲ **9.** Turn the wall. If the piece is moist, use a loop tool; if dry, use a large trimming tool. Keep checking the thickness as you work. If the piece tends to deform, let it dry for another day.

▼ **11.** When you turn the neck, position the tool so that it fits the contours of the piece. If the tool doesn't fit the vessel as you move it up and down, rotate it at strategic points to make it conform.

You can work the neck with smaller flexible ribs, but don't use them on the whole piece because they will leave ridges. It's best to use a large metal rib for the body of the piece since it will leave fewer marks.

▼ **12.** Once the piece has been turned, go over it with a slightly damp sponge and let it dry upside down, if possible, for one more day. The base is the part of the vase that takes the longest to dry, so it's best to turn it later. Large pieces are usually turned in several stages.

▲ **13.** Turn the piece in the chuck once again, making sure the base is flat and parallel to the wheel. Make a recessed ring.

Vases, like teapots, usually don't have raised foot rings, in order to keep them more stable.

Using the small loop tool, make a circle about an inch and a half from the edge of the base. Hollow out the inside of the circle. To smooth off the lowered area, use a piece of flexible rib. Go over it with a sponge and let it dry.

▶ **14.** Throughout the turning process, keep an eye on the thickness of the piece. With this shape it's no problem to determine the thickness of the walls, since you can get your hand inside. But if you were working with a narrow-necked vase, you would hold it by the base with your left hand.

▶ **15.** Transfer it to your right hand. If you repeat this several times, you'll be able to tell where the greatest weight lies in the piece, at the base or the top. You'll have to thin the part where you've detected the extra weight. If you feel the weight is evenly distributed, then you can turn the piece from top to bottom.

Turning vases with long, thin necks

In order to turn a vase with a long, thin neck, you'll have to make a taller chuck than normal to keep the neck from touching the bottom of the chuck and becoming deformed.

▶ **1.** Make a tall chuck and check to be sure that the neck will not touch the bottom.

▶ **2.** Center the vase upside down and turn the base slightly to reduce its diameter.

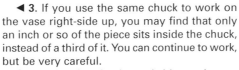

◀ **3.** If you use the same chuck to work on the vase right-side up, you may find that only an inch or so of the piece sits inside the chuck, instead of a third of it. You can continue to work, but be very careful.

Center the piece by the neck. It's very important that the neck be centered well to keep the piece from turning out lopsided.

▶ **4.** Turn the vase, making sure the neck is centered. If necessary, cut the rim to make it parallel to the wheel. Every time the vase moves off center, re-center it by the neck.

▲ 5. Shape the contour with a wire loop tool.

► 7. To finish, go over the piece with a flexible rib, and then with a nearly dry sponge and let the piece dry right-side up for another day.

▼ 8. On the next day, finish turning the base and make the foot.

▲ 6. Hold the piece by the base with your right hand so that the opening is level with your ear. Tap it with the tip of your index finger from top to bottom. If the sound is high-pitched, this means the walls are thin; and if it's low-pitched, they are thick; in that case, you'll have to lighten them. If the sound is even, the piece must be the same thickness throughout. Then repeat the operation while you're turning, checking the base at the same time; for if it's thin, you'll hear the high-pitched sound clearly. At first it will be difficult to distinguish the sounds.

► 9. The piece can dry on any surface, but plaster is best, since the piece will dry more slowly at the base, and it will dry more uniformly.

Turning closed forms

To turn a closed form properly, you have to cut it perfectly parallel to the wheel once it's done, since this will be the only point of reference for centering it on the chuck.

Before turning, center the piece so that the base is once again parallel to the wheel. Scribe a line parallel to the base in the middle of the piece. When you turn the piece over to turn the top, this line will serve as a reference point for centering the piece. That way, you will always turn a piece that's centered.

▲ **1.** Place the closed form upside down on the chuck, center it by the base, and remove the rough edge.

▲ **2.** Reduce the diameter of the base and use a needle tool to scribe a line around the middle of the body.

◄ **3.** Turn the piece over and center it so that the line indicated by the finger in the photo is parallel to the wheel.

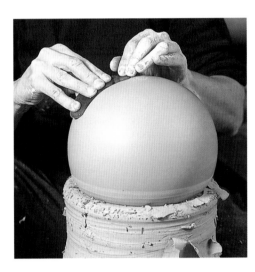

► **4.** Turn the piece and go over it with a flexible rib.

▼ **5.** If there's a mark between the turned and unturned parts, it can serve as a reference for centering the closed form when you turn it over. Otherwise, you'll have to make another mark with the needle tool. Turn the piece to adjust its shape, and finish off the base.

▼ **6.** Once the base is finished, puncture it with a thin needle tool again, as the original hole may have closed up during the turning process. Don't let the piece dry without a hole for the air trapped inside to escape; otherwise the piece will crack.

▼ **7.** Place the piece on a bat and let it dry.

Plates

I f you have mastered throwing the three basic pieces—the bowl, the cylinder, and the vase—you should find it quite easy to throw a plate. But turning it in such a way that it functions properly is somewhat labor intensive.

In this section you'll find various ways of making saucers, plates, platters, and other serving dishes, so that everyone can learn the easiest way to make each piece.

Plates can be thrown in various ways: with wider or narrower bases, or larger or smaller outer rings; on a bat, or directly on the wheel. But the factors that determine the shape will be the nature of the clay, its shrinkage during drying, and possible deformation in the kiln.

It will be helpful to observe the types of plates used for various purposes and note the small differences among them that distinguish one from another.

Throwing plates off a hump

Saucers, which are normally between 4¹/₂ and 6 inches in diameter, are usually the only plates made off the hump. You have to figure the size of the saucer according to the type of cup it will hold; the handle will be contained within the saucer, and that determines the size.

This is the fastest method for throwing plates, and it should be used whenever possible to streamline your work.

If the clay allows, you can even throw larger plates with this method. Many ceramists use this method to throw dinner plates.

▲ To keep the outer ring of a plate from drooping while throwing, the bottom of the wall should be somewhat thicker than the rest of the ring, with the thinnest point at the outer rim.

► **1.** Center the clay in a cone and press hard on the top.

▼ **4.** Select the clay as you did with the bowl (see pages 38–39). Up to this point, this exercise is the same as throwing a bowl, except that the cone is a bit wider.

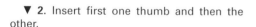

▼ **2.** Insert first one thumb and then the other.

▼ **3.** Then press outward on the inside edge of the hole.

▲ **5.** Press on the clay with your left hand, placing four fingers on the inside and your thumb on the outside to thin the wall. The index or middle finger will actually do most of the work.

Press with the right index and middle fingers, and keep your thumbs joined. Draw your hands toward you horizontally from the center to thin the walls.

▲ **6.** Once you have achieved a flat base and slightly curved walls, cut off the outer edge with a needle tool. It's very important to cut it well, since this will form the reference point for centering the piece.

▲ **7.** Cut the piece off at the base with a cotton string, just as with a bowl. If you quickly stretch the string taut with your right hand and reduce the speed of the wheel, the plate will remain on the cone because of the width of the base. Stop the wheel, remove the plate with your index fingers and thumbs, and place it on a bat.

Turning a small plate

The previous piece will be turned later on. To illustrate the turning process we have chosen a different plate so you can see another shape; the turning process is the same.

▶ **1.** First make a cone, then a small hole, and flatten the base.

▶ **2.** Use the needle tool to cut off the top of the cone parallel to the base. If you can't get it perfectly parallel, it should be slightly concave rather than convex.

▶ **3.** Cut off the outside edge.

▶ **4.** Dry the top with a heat gun. Dry it just enough so that the clay of the chuck doesn't stick to the piece. If the chuck is too dry, the piece will move when it's turned.

▲ 5. Center the piece, holding it by the outer rim. If the plate was not cut properly, cut it now with a needle tool. Otherwise, every time you center the plate, it will be different, and it will turn out uneven.

▲ 6. Flatten the base with a flexible rib. This tool works very well on large surfaces and can be used on all sorts of plates, including this small one.

▶ 7. Add contour to the piece with a wire loop tool.

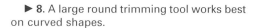

▶ 8. A large round trimming tool works best on curved shapes.

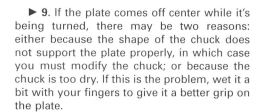

▶ 9. If the plate comes off center while it's being turned, there may be two reasons: either because the shape of the chuck does not support the plate properly, in which case you must modify the chuck; or because the chuck is too dry. If this is the problem, wet it a bit with your fingers to give it a better grip on the plate.

◀ 10. With a flexible rib, define the contour.

▶ 11. Before you make the foot ring, center the piece again. If the base is not centered with respect to the outer rim of the plate, then it was not turned correctly. If this is the case, it's better to center the outside rim of the base and then make the foot ring with a uniform width. Once it's centered, mark out the foot ring with a small trimming tool.

▲ **12.** Hollow out the inside of the base and flatten it properly. Go over it with a slightly damp sponge and leave it to dry face down.

▲ **13.** Next, open up the chuck so that the foot ring can fit inside without being damaged.

▲ **14.** Center the piece on the outer edge and work the inside. Lower the edge and make it slightly curved.

▼ **15.** Then go over it with a piece of flexible rib to smooth it.

▼ **16.** Work the center of the piece. If it's intended to hold a cup, it should be flat. If not, then it can be somewhat curved.

▼ **17.** Go over the piece with a nearly dry sponge.

▶ **18.** Place the piece on a bat to dry.

▶ **19.** This piece has the same shape as the previous one, but it was turned differently, with turning ridges on the inside. Small variations in the finish provide different results in these two plates.

Saucers with a ring

Most saucers intended to hold a cup have a small inner ridge. Many restaurants use a single type of saucer for all their cups, so they usually aren't the same size as the base of the cup. That procedure saves inventory, but the cups and saucers move around when you pick them up, since the saucers often deform during firing and are not flat enough.

Ridges can be made at the time of throwing or turning.

Making a ridge at the time of throwing

It's important to know the degree of shrinkage of the type of clay used so that the ridge will be just the right size for the base of the cup when it's done, unless both pieces are made at the same time.

◄ **1.** Center a cone of clay and press hard on the top. Open a hole.

◄ **2.** With your right thumb in the middle of the flat surface and your middle finger underneath, apply pressure to draw the clay outward. Use your left thumb as well, even though the right hand does most of the work.

▲ **3.** With the four fingers of your left hand on the inside and your left thumb on the outside, squeeze the clay to thin it out and draw it toward you. At the same time, use your right index and thumb to squeeze the wall against the remaining three fingers as the hands work together.

▶ **4.** Work on the ridge to give it the desired height and diameter, then shape the plate.

▼ **5.** Cut the outer edge with a needle tool and remove any rough edges.

Making the ridge by turning

Sometimes you can make the ridge when you turn the piece, since that allows you to study a very small surface area and decide how you want it to be. Once you've had a good look, if you need to make many saucers, it may be better to make the ridge from the outset as you throw the pieces, in order to save time.

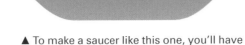

▲ To make a saucer like this one, you'll have to make it thicker than normal when throwing.

▲ **1.** Flatten the base of the first saucer.

▼ Keep in mind that the upper part will be hollowed out somewhat to make the area for the cup to fit into, and the bottom will be hollowed out as well to make a raised foot ring. The success of a piece like this depends on a uniform thickness of the walls, so that when the piece shrinks, deformation and cracking are minimized.

▼ **2.** Turn it over so it's face up.

▲ **3.** Center it, holding it by the edges.

▲ **4.** Hollow out the center and make it flat.

▼ **5.** Go over it with a flexible rib so that the center is flat. For the cup to sit correctly on the saucer, both pieces must be parallel; that is, the center of the saucer and the foot on the cup's base must be flat.

◀ **6.** Then add the final contours to the outer ring and finish off the piece.

▶ The center should be hollowed out flat, whereas the outer rim can be flat (A) or curved (B).

The ridge can also be made by turning down the inner surface of the saucer; but as we have seen, it's quicker to make it when you throw the piece (C).

If you don't want to make an inside ridge by turning, the piece should be thrown somewhat thinner (D).

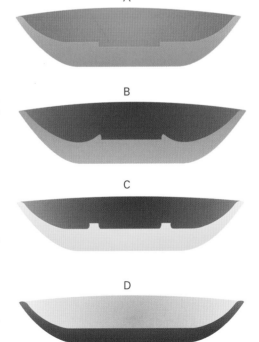

A

B

C

D

Dinner and dessert plates

Dinner plates are usually eight to ten inches in diameter, and dessert plates normally have a diameter of about seven inches. Calculate a shrinkage of 10 to 15 percent, depending on the type of clay used, and add this amount to the desired dimensions.

This piece should be done on a bat, unless you can handle a piece this large and the type of clay permits it.

► **1.** Center the clay on a bat and open a hole.

▲ **2.** Pull the clay toward you as you press down on it.

▼ **3.** Work on the base with your fingertips to flatten it.

▼ **4.** Pull the clay toward you. It's very important to press hard on the base, since otherwise this type of piece tends to crack in the center as it dries.

▼ **5.** Continue drawing the clay toward you, and then finish off by adding a curve at the edge, or shaping it as desired.

▼ **6.** Cut around the edge with a needle tool.

▼ **7.** Remove any rough edges remaining from the cut.

◀ **8.** Stop the wheel and cut a third of the way under the plate with a wire or nylon line. Finish the cut with the wheel running and the wire held taut. That will cut the piece off nicely; set it aside to dry.

▶ **9.** Don't turn the plate when it's too moist and susceptible to deforming at the rim. Use the same type of chuck as for saucers, but with a slightly larger hole. For the piece to be supported correctly, the walls of the chuck should be at least 1½ to 2 inches thick, and the chuck should be ½ inch smaller in diameter than the plate.

▶ **10.** Center the piece by the outer rim and flatten it with a flexible angle tool.

▶ **11.** Next, reduce the diameter of the base.

▼ **12.** Use a small trimming tool to mark the ridge, and then hollow out the inside.

▼ **13.** Then flatten the base with a flexible rib or a trimming tool.

▲ **14.** Go over it with a slightly damp sponge. This plate has a recessed ring, which is not usual in plates, since they normally have a raised foot ring like many lighter pieces.

▲ **15.** Starting with the same plate, make a line about 1¹/₂ inches on the outside of the previous one and remove the extra clay. You can see that this type of plate is lighter, as more clay has been removed in modifying the foot.

▲ **16.** Finally, go over the plate with a sponge and allow to dry face down on a bat.

▼ **18.** Turn the rim of the piece and leave the rest as is, with marks from your fingers.

◄ **17.** Take the same chuck and open it up some more. If you dried it too much with the heat gun, you won't be able to modify it. You have to make it so that the opening is larger than the foot of the plate.

▼ **19.** Next, allow to dry on a clean bat.

► **20.** Small variations in plates can provide for a great variety of forms.

▼ **21.** Below are two types of soup bowl, variations on the cylinder and the bowl.

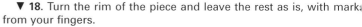

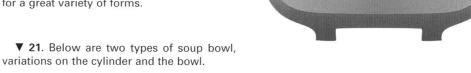

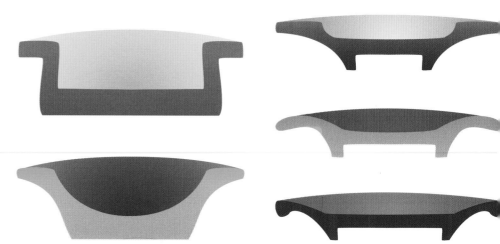

Another way to make plates or platters

Plates can also be made using the technique shown on these pages. This is normally used to make pieces with slightly raised rims, as in a platter or flat serving dish. The piece shown here is about fourteen inches in diameter. To turn it, you will have to turn it over repeatedly to create the right contours and thickness. When that part's done, the inside should be finished, and then the outside, using the same chuck.

▲ **1.** Center the clay on a bat, making sure it's flat. With your right palm, press downward and away from the center, while flattening it with your left thumb. Both hands work together.

▲ **2.** You can also flatten it with your left palm and your right fingertips, moving outward from the center and in opposite directions.

▲ **3.** Once the clay is the right size, cut the rim off with a wooden tool in the case of a plaster bat, or with a needle tool in the case of any other type of bat. If the strip doesn't come off, hold the tool flat and insert it between the clay and the bat to complete the cut.

▲ **4.** Next put your fingers under the outside edge and lift the clay up a little.

▲ **5.** Shape the walls by pressing with your index fingers.

▼ **6.** Then cut the base, or if it's a thin piece, wait until it loosens by itself. Remove it from the wheel and allow to dry.

▼ **7.** When the piece is hard enough to keep its shape, prepare a chuck and dry the top with a heat gun.

▼ **8.** Place the platter face down, center it, and flatten it with an angle tool. You can use this tool to flatten the entire base.

◄ 9. You can also use a flexible rectangular rib to flatten the base; but because of its small size it won't cover the entire surface, and it's used only to flatten the area where the foot ring will be.

► 10. Reduce the base.

▲ 11. Adjust the contours with a flexible rib and turn the piece over before you make the foot ring.

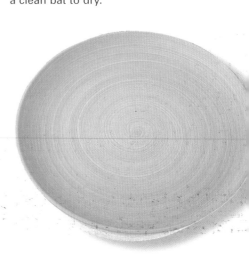

▲ 12. Then place the platter face up on the chuck and center it.

▲ 13. Work on flattening the inside.

► 15. Smooth the piece off with a flexible rib, working continually from the center to the outside so the shape is free of noticeable ridges.

▼ 16. Turn the outside and inside edges with a wire loop tool.

► 14. Next, shape the curve on the side.

▼ 17. Go over the piece with a sponge, working outward from the center. Allow to dry face up.

▼ 18. Remove from the wheel and place on a clean bat to dry.

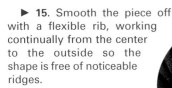

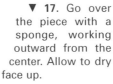

▲ **19.** When it has dried somewhat, turn the plate over and make the foot ring. You can use the same chuck without modifying it.

▲ **20.** Draw two circles to indicate the inner and outer edges of the foot ring.

▲ **21.** Hollow out the large area inside the inner circle with a loop tool. If the clay is very soft, the tool may dig in.

▲ **22.** If this happens, correct it with a small trimming tool.

▲ **23.** Relieve the ring by removing clay from the outside.

▼ **26.** Finally, go over the piece with a sponge and let it dry face down on a clean bat.

► **24.** If you get chatter marks during the turning process, work with a different tool.

► **25.** Chatter marks can be removed with a wire loop tool, or you can wait until the piece dries some more and go over the area with a flexible rib, moving in the direction opposite to the bumps.

Casseroles

asseroles were traditionally made using the following procedure. Today, they are usually made in factories rather than by hand.

If you want to make a casserole for cooking, you must use heat-resistant clay; otherwise it will break when you put it on the stove. This piece should be made on a bat.

The mug shown in the left-hand margin doesn't have a flat base and wobbles like a top. It's part of a series by the author called nonutilitarian ceramics. *It was also made following the method described below, as are amphoras. If the base is left thicker than shown here, you can use the extra clay to continue shaping the piece once you turn it over. This process may help us create new forms.*

▲ 1. Center the piece on a bat.

▲ 2. Insert first one thumb and then the other.

▲ 3. Then use both hands to enlarge the hole and deepen it down to the bat.

▼ 4. Work the clay out of the base, squeezing the clay to pull it up. Avoid pulling it off the base, and leave a little to support the piece.

◄ 5. Draw in the rim the same way you did with the vase. Begin with your right middle, ring, and little fingers held straight.

► 6. Continue working with those three fingers bent. Move your hands toward the center.

▲ **7.** Round the piece by pulling the clay up with the cupped fingers of the left hand.

▲ **8.** Neck the piece again . . .

▲ **9.** . . . until just a small opening remains.

◀ **10.** Place one hand inside the piece again. The hole is small, but it's flexible enough to get your hand in. Check from the base up to be sure the walls are right and there are no ridges inside.

▶ **11.** Finally, close the piece up as if you were making a closed form.

▲ **12.** Pinch the remaining tip until it comes off.

▼ **13.** Press on the top to compress the clay and keep it from cracking.

▶ **14.** Continue to press on different areas to achieve the desired shape, then cut it off the base. Allow to dry for half a day. It's important to cut the piece off, since you need to continue working on it before it becomes so dry that it loosens from the bat by itself.

▲ **15.** Before the piece has gotten hard enough to turn, make a chuck.

▲ **16.** The upper edge of the chuck should be made thick.

▲ **17.** Cut out the inner rim and dry the are that will contact the piece.

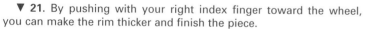

▲ **19.** Then carefully wet the rim of the piece and begin working on it.

▲ **20.** Level the rim by cutting it with needle tool.

◄ **18.** Next, center the piece face up.

▼ **21.** By pushing with your right index finger toward the wheel, you can make the rim thicker and finish the piece.

▼ **22.** If you prefer, you can make a thinner rim by pulling the clay upward.

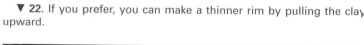

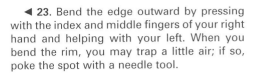

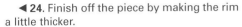

◄ **23.** Bend the edge outward by pressing with the index and middle fingers of your right hand and helping with your left. When you bend the rim, you may trap a little air; if so, poke the spot with a needle tool.

◄ **24.** Finish off the piece by making the rim a little thicker.

▼ **26.** The rim of this piece was not finished by throwing, but rather by turning.

► **25.** Remove from the wheel and allow to dry.

◄ Pieces the author made with the technique shown here. These pieces were made the same way as the others, but with a different shape.

▼ The rim of this cup was bent as described in steps 23 and 24.

▼ Another type of vessel.

Goblets

*T*he main characteristic of a goblet is that the cup is separated from the stem by a wall. This piece must be thrown in two stages; the first part is thrown and then allowed to dry for a day before continuing with the next. The base of the first piece needs to be soft in order to form the best possible joint. If you forcefully dig your fingertip into the clay of the base and push it to one side, the clay should move; if it doesn't, it's too dry.

To make this piece, it's essential to control the amount of moisture in the piece. If water gets onto the first piece as it dries, it could crack later. Excess moisture could cause the piece to stick to the chuck and become deformed.

There are several different methods for making goblets, depending on their shape and size. Three different methods are explained below.

Throwing the second piece on a separate wheel

This procedure is used when the second part of the goblet is as large as the first one. If available, a second wheel is used to make the second part. If you don't have access to another wheel, invert the order and make the second part first.

◄ **1.** First, throw one part of the goblet, usually the larger of the two parts. In the photo, you can see a bowl, a small cylinder and a large one. Allow them to dry until the rim doesn't bend easily. Just before it's hard enough to turn, you can resume working.

◄ **2.** Put some clay onto the wheel and open it down to the bottom, making sure that the outer circumference of the chuck is a little smaller than the piece you're making. Make the rim thick so you can cut it with a potter's needle to get the right diameter and thickness. It's important to make the chuck properly so that the piece is supported well and doesn't move when it's turned.

▲ **3.** Cut the outer rim at an angle.

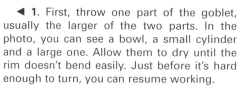

► **4.** Now cut the rim perpendicular to the wheel to refine the rim. This insures that the chuck will be perfectly centered, since the piece will be held by the outside.

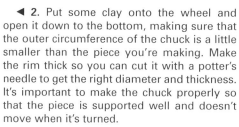

◄ **5.** Cut off the top, and if you wish, the inner part, although in this case that's not necessary, since the inside won't be used. Steps 3, 4, and 5 can be done in any order.

► **6.** Then dry the chuck with a heat gun. Don't dry it for too long; just fifteen seconds is adequate in most cases. Before you turn the piece, it's important to feel it to see how it's made and detect any variations in thickness.

▲ 7. Place the cup of the goblet on the chuck face down and center it by the rim. Cut down the base to the desired dimensions while the clay is soft, removing it with a wire loop tool.

If the base is very thick, it can be thinned now, since some pieces made in this way cannot be thinned later. If the base is too thin it will collapse during throwing later on. Here there's no problem because we're dealing with a bowl shape, which can be thinned on the inside at any time.

▲ 8. With the wheel in motion, scribe several circles on the base with a needle tool, within a ½-inch-wide strip in the area where the base is to be joined. Then scribe some curves within this ½ inch.

▲ 9. Stop the wheel. Add some slip to the scored area and measure the outside diameter with a compass. If the slip dries right away, add more to keep it soft. Before adding the second part, make sure the slip appears dull, not shiny, so that it adheres well without sliding.

▲ 10. On another wheel, if available, make the second part. Otherwise, make this piece before you make the chuck. Center the clay and open a hole down to the wheel head. Draw the clay to form either a cylinder or a cone, depending on the piece you're making. Make the rim thicker and adjust the piece to the measurement taken previously.

Don't throw this piece too thin, since it will be worked some more when it's attached to the other piece.

▶ 13. The rim should match the scored area for the pieces to join correctly. Center the second piece on top of the first and press the outside edge onto the piece.

▶ 14. Then press on the inner edge to reinforce it. If the joint is too thin, work the clay in the direction opposite to the usual, i.e. downward, to even out the thickness of the wall.

▲ 11. If you cut into the rim the cross section would look like this. The important thing is that the clay be evenly distributed, without excessively thick areas in the base, so that the work is easier once the two pieces are joined.

▲ 12. Cut off the finished piece, turn it over, and place it onto the base of the first piece.

▶ **17.** Remove the piece carefully, making sure the mouth retains its shape. If the mouth deforms when you take the piece off the chuck, fix it before letting it dry. Cover the lower part with plastic and allow to dry for one day. Only when both parts are equally moist can you turn the piece.

▲ **15.** Once the two parts are joined, carefully and gently pull the clay up.

▲ **16.** Cut the rim parallel to the wheel.

When the second part is very small

You can use this process when the second part of the goblet is smaller than the first part.

It can also be used in other instances, such as when a rim breaks. In that case, the coil that's used should be smaller.

Ceramists who are making a number of the same pieces don't normally use a coil. Instead, they throw pieces off the hump and join them.

Some ceramists find it easier to use a coil when they don't have to make so many pieces. Just be sure that no water gets into the piece when adding the coil to the base; otherwise the two parts won't adhere properly.

◀ **1.** Place the small cylinder on the chuck. Flatten the base, thinning it as needed. The piece to be turned is small, so the base can also be thinned later if necessary.

▲ **2.** Adjust the contours with a wire loop tool. Don't turn the piece at this time, simply adjust the contours somewhat. If you turn it now, the walls will be too thin to turn the whole goblet once the two pieces have been joined.

▶ **3.** Score it with a needle tool and add some slip, as with the previous piece.

▼ **4.** Make a coil by hand and place it on the scored area.

▼ **5.** Coil it around so that one end overlaps the other, and cut off the excess.

▼ **6.** Press the coil onto the base along the outside.

▲ **7.** Then do the same around he inside.

▲ **8.** Throw it, pressing on the joint to make it adhere well.

◄ **9.** Throw from bottom to top, distributing the clay and shaping the piece as desired. Remove from the wheel and cover the lower part with plastic as on the previous piece. If it doesn't come out right the first time, cut off the added part with a needle tool and make it again with softer clay, again preparing the base with slip.

When the second part continues the shape of the first

If you want to make a piece where the joint s invisible, the joint should be located on the ide.

This process gives the piece a sort of nagical air in which the outer appearnce has nothing to do with the inner tructure.

If the second part is to have the ame shape as the first, it should be nade a fraction of an inch wider; he first piece is drier and won't hrink as much as the second one, vhich has yet to begin drying. You can lso make the second part thicker and hin it out by turning it.

It's best to make the first part larger than the econd so that the joint isn't in the middle of he piece and it can be used either side up, providing two receptacles of different sizes.

Before joining the two parts, make the base he proper thickness. If the base is left too hick, the piece will be too heavy and you von't be able to thin it later. If, on the other hand, it's too thin, it may collapse when it's urned. Because the joint is made to one side, t's less likely to collapse than if it were in the center of the piece.

▶ **5.** Next, place it onto the first piece and press the rim against the scored area of the ase. If this area becomes too thin, you can einforce it by pressing the clay downward so t doesn't turn out too fragile. Once the hickness has been adjusted, pull the clay up o distribute it evenly.

◄ **2.** Score the area with a needle tool and add some slip.

▶ **3.** On another wheel, make another piece just like the one in step 10 (page 111) of the first piece, but make the rim thicker.

◄ **1.** Center the piece on the chuck and flatten the base, thinning it if necessary. Remove some clay from the outer rim of the base with a wire loop tool to make a step the same size as the rim of the piece to be joined. This is one case where the base has to be thinned to the right dimensions because you can't do it later.

◄ **4.** Adjust it to the measurement taken and cut it off.

▼ **6.** Finish the piece off, continuing the preestablished shape. Remove from the wheel and cover with plastic. Allow to dry until both parts are equally moist.

Turning goblets

If you want to perfect the shape of a goblet, you can turn it when both parts have the right degree of dryness, just as with any other piece.

If one of the two parts is drier than the other before turning, cover the vessel with plastic and allow to dry for at least a day so that one part absorbs the excess moisture from the other and the two parts become uniform.

Don't turn a piece if both parts aren't uniformly moist. Otherwise, the proportions will differ from when the piece was made, and in some cases the shape will be different, to the detriment of the finished piece.

If you have to turn several pieces, begin with the smallest, as smaller pieces tend to dry more quickly.

▲ **1.** Place the piece on a chuck. The chuck for turning this goblet should be conical and can have a small hole. If it has a large hole, the chuck may be too weak, causing it to come off center during turning.

▲ **2.** Next, center the piece on the larger part. If it works to use the other part, always line it up at the same place. Otherwise the piece would be worked differently every time it was removed from the wheel.

▼ **3.** Turn the walls, first with a trimming tool or a wire loop tool, and then with flexible metal ribs. If you want to thin the base a little, you can use a flexible rib, working perpendicular to the rim.

▲ **4.** Bevel the inner edge of the rim.

▲ **5.** Bevel the outer edge.

► **6.** If you have made the chuck in such a way that you can turn the piece over, you can continue to use it. Even if it's not as steady, it may be adequate.

▼ **8.** Finally, go over the piece with a slightly damp sponge, remove it from the wheel, and allow it to dry uncovered.

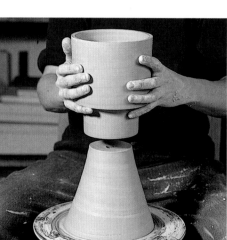

▲ **7.** Bevel the edges with a wire loop tool. If the rim is fairly thick, you can disguise it by thinning it with a flexible rib, working perpendicular to the rim. This piece doesn't need to be turned on the inside.

► **9.** Modify the chuck, center the piece, and turn it using the same method.

▲ **10.** Turn over and finish the rim. If you wish, turn the inside using flexible ribs.

▲ **11.** The third piece can be turned using the same procedure. If the shrinkage was not calculated right, turn the entire piece so that it's slightly conical; that way it will scarcely be noticeable.

▼ **13.** Allow the pieces to dry on clean bats. Keep an eye on the pieces as they dry. Some pieces may look perfect when freshly turned, but upon examination the next day, after drying, you can see the defects. Flexible tools work very well to correct defects in clay that's fairly dry, but they leave scratches or bumps if used on wet clay.

► **12.** Adjust the shape with a flexible rib, finish off the rim, and go over the piece with a sponge.

► If the base is very narrow, you can add stability by making the base thicker and heavier.

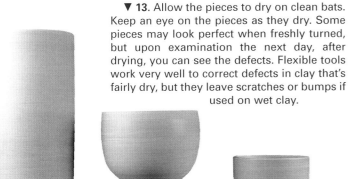

▼ The stems of these goblets were made from coils.

▼ Relief was added to these goblets when they were turned.

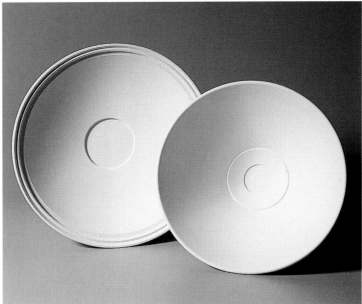

Two-piece vases

If you want to make a large piece and the clay you're working with is so soft that it collapses, you can make it in two parts.

The basic procedure is to make the lower part of the piece, allow it to dry, and then make the upper part. If the piece is very large, you may have to repeat the process several times. This system of joining two pieces allows you to control the shape and provide continuity, making it look like a single piece. Depending on the type of piece, the joint is either on the upper or lower part.

Not all ceramists follow this procedure to make such pieces. Some make the lower part using this technique, but finish the upper part with coils. For an understanding of the coiling method, see the step-by-step instructions on pages 135–136.

Joining at the top

Before beginning to work, consider the piece you intend to make. If it's very wide, you should throw it on a bat. If it's narrow, you can throw it directly on the wheel.

You must have perfect control over the amount of water you use to make a piece like this. Too much water will make the piece and the chuck stick to one another, and usually you can't separate them without damaging the piece.

► **2.** Make a chuck that accommodates half or two-thirds of the piece inside it and holds it firmly in place so it doesn't move when turned. If the piece should move, all your work could be ruined.

◄ **1.** Throw the lower part on a bat and cut it off at the base.

Then allow to dry for half a day or a day, depending on the clay and the room temperature. Before the piece is ready to turn, that is when the rim can be bent only slightly, continue working very carefully to avoid deforming it.

▲ **3.** Cut the inner and upper edges of the chuck's rim with a needle tool, then dry it with the electric heat gun.

► **4.** Center the piece in the chuck and moisten the rim with slip.

▲ **5.** Make a cone on another wheel. Make the rim thicker, then flatten it, and make a groove all the way around so it will fit onto the other piece.

◄ 6. Cut off the cone you've just turned, and as you hold it by the lower part, which is the thickest, place it on the piece in the chuck without touching the rim with your hands.

▼ 7. Next, center the piece and press the rim down onto the first piece you made, first from the outside, then from the inside and the outside at the same time.

◄ 9. Remove from the chuck and allow to dry.

▲ 8. Then pull the clay up and shape the piece.

► 10. When the piece is ready to be turned, make a chuck and put the piece onto it face down. Flatten the base with an angle tool, since this surface is larger than the previous ones.

▼ 11. Since the clay is soft, use a wire loop tool to reduce the diameter of the base so you can use the same chuck to turn both sides of the piece.

► 12. Turn the vase over and center it by the neck. Turn the walls with a trimming tool. If the tool skips or leaves bumps on the surface, the clay is too soft and you should use a wire loop tool.

► **13.** With a flexible rib, work on the neck and unify the shape.

◄ **14.** Finally, go over the piece with a sponge.

▼ **15.** Modify the chuck so it's narrower, because the base wasn't reduced properly and the chuck needs to be changed.

▼ **16.** Turn the base and blend the shape into the rest of the piece.

▼ **17.** Then make the foot ring and hollow out the area inside it.

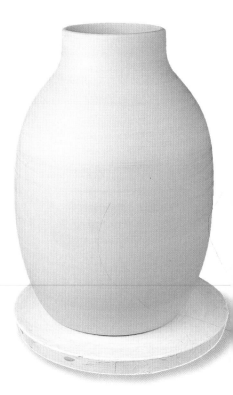

◄ **18.** Go over the piece with a sponge to smooth it.

► **19.** Next, place it on a bat to dry.

Joining at the lower part

Some pieces are too unstable to throw as previously described, since the lower part is narrower than the top. For these pieces, the upper part must be thrown first, and then the joint is made on the base of the first part. The following is a description of how this works.

▶ **1.** Since we're using a clay with high porcelain content, we have thrown the first part on a bat. Make a cylinder slightly wider at the base. You will actually make a ball shape.

▶ **2.** Distribute the clay evenly throughout the walls.

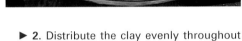

◀ **3.** Then draw in the neck.

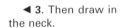

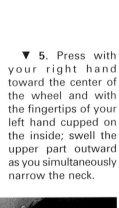

◀ **4.** Shape the piece, applying outward pressure with your left hand on the inside while supporting it firmly with your right hand on the outside as the walls become thinner.

▼ **5.** Press with your right hand toward the center of the wheel and with the fingertips of your left hand cupped on the inside; swell the upper part outward as you simultaneously narrow the neck.

▼ **6.** Continue closing up the neck.

◀ **8.** Finish by closing up the neck, using the little finger of your left hand to press on the clay from the inside.

◀ **7.** Check the thickness of the piece to make sure there are no ridges, and adjust the thickness of the walls.

▶ **9.** Then close up the neck more, squeezing the clay from the outside.

◀ **10.** Cut the tip of the neck off with a needle tool.

▶ **11.** Cut the piece off at the base, as you will have to handle it before it comes loose by itself. Remove from the wheel and allow to dry for half a day or a day, depending on the room temperature.

◀ **12.** When the piece is still a little too moist for turning, make a chuck large enough to hold half of the piece inside it. Place the piece face down in it and center it.

▶ **13.** Remove the rough edge from around the base.

► **14.** Cut out the base with a needle tool, unless you threw it without a base, making the hole all the way down to the wheel. Sometimes it's best not to make the hole right through to the wheel, since the base provides support and preserves the shape when you handle the piece.

▼ **16.** Level the clay and make a ring as if you were forming a neck.

▲ **15.** Moisten the area for the joint.

▲ **17.** Measure the outside diameter.

► **18.** On another wheel, throw the piece to be joined to the first one.

▼ **19.** Flatten the clay and make the rim thicker.

▼ **20.** Make a groove around the rim the same size as the measurement taken from the other piece.

◄ 21. Cut off the piece you've just thrown and place it onto the first one. Make the opening wider as you distribute the clay and draw it upward.

► 22. Center the piece well.

◄ 23. Turn the walls near the top, evening out the thickness, and begin forming a neck.

◄ 24. Next, close up the neck, as if you were throwing a regular vase with a narrow neck.

▼ 25. Squeeze the neck to compress the clay as you move your hands toward the center.

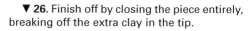

▼ 26. Finish off by closing the piece entirely, breaking off the extra clay in the tip.

▼ 27. Then work on the base, perhaps lowering the center, as with a foot. You need to press hard when you close up the piece at the base, since it could crack if not done properly.

◄ **28.** Go over the walls with a rib to smooth them and remove slip.

► **29.** As it can't be placed upside down, this piece must be set onto a bat until it's hard enough to be turned over. The bat used should not be too hard. If it is, cover it with something soft. The first piece that was thrown is still a little damp, and a hard bat could easily dig in and leave marks. The same chuck that was used to throw the piece is used here.

◄ **31.** Then turn the lower part.

▼ **30.** When both parts of the piece are equally hard, you can turn it. Begin turning, centering it by the mouth.

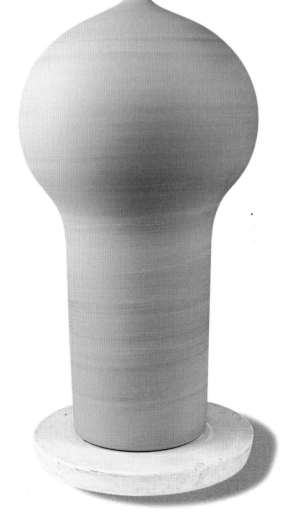

► **32.** Once the piece is finished, allow to dry on a bat.

Centerpieces

*C*enterpieces are large, low pieces that can be used for a variety of purposes, from utilitarian to decorative.

When you make this kind of piece, you usually don't think about the shape you're going to make, but about the effort involved in working on such a large piece. If you're familiar with the fundamental throwing techniques, these pieces should pose no problem beyond the strength they require. Just the same, you should plan the shape of the piece beforehand to avoid unnecessarily thick areas.

Below we'll consider several of these pieces, analyzed according to their shape to facilitate throwing them.

Any method is valid if it allows you to achieve the desired results. Hence, several methods are described so that you can practice with the one you consider the easiest.

Centerpieces based on the cylinder

These are pieces with a flat base and perpendicular walls. As you can see, this piece has a wide base and low walls.

For this type of piece, you need to apply lots of pressure to the base to keep it from cracking during the drying process. At first it's better to make pieces with thick bases so you have enough clay to level them properly.

These pieces are thrown on bats. Because of the force needed to make such pieces, the bed of clay between the wheel and the bat should cover the entire surface of the wheel and be made of fairly soft clay to keep the bat in place. See step one in "Bats."

◄ **1.** Place a large, low lump of clay on a bat and center it. Open a hole and widen it pressing downward and toward you with both hands.

▶ **2.** Work on the base with your fingertips to make it perfectly flat.

◄ **3.** You can also work with your right index finger hooked over your thumb, turning your wrist as you press with your left hand.

◄ **4.** When the entire base is quite flat, pull up the walls, squeezing with your right index and middle fingers and moving upward while you keep your left hand on the rim so it doesn't widen.

▶ **5.** With the fingertips of your left hand on the inside and your right thumb wrapped around your index finger on the outside, press the clay at the base of the wall to make a right angle and pull the clay upward.

▲ **6.** Adjust the thickness of the walls as you pull the clay up.

▲ **7.** Cut the rim and remove the rough edges left after the cut, and then see how it looks, since this piece will not be turned. Cut it off the bat or wait until it comes loose by itself.

▲ **8.** When the piece is fairly dry but the base can still be worked, you can turn the piece. Since you'll turn only the base of this piece, you can wait until the piece is a little drier than usual. Make a chuck with a thick, slanted wall the same size as the rim of the piece to be turned.

▲ **9.** Measure the inside diameter of the rim with a compass.

▶ **10.** Check that the chuck will fit the piece.

▼ **12.** Cut the upper edge of the rim parallel to the wheel.

▼ **13.** Clean up the outer edge.

▲ **11.** Cut the rim at an angle with a needle tool and remove the strip of clay.

▼ **14.** Dry the chuck a little more than usual with the heat gun to keep it from deforming under the heavy piece.

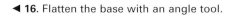

◄ **16.** Flatten the base with an angle tool.

▼ **17.** Mark off the foot ring about ¹/₂ to ³/₄ inch from the edge of the base.

▲ **15.** Place the piece face down on the chuck and center it as you hold it by the walls. Once it's centered, make sure the rim is parallel to the wheel.

▼ **18.** Hollow out the area inside this circle with a wire loop tool.

▲ **19.** If you prefer, you can also do this with a trimming tool.

▶ **20.** Leave the marks produced by the polishing tool to preserve the relief on the walls. Next, go over it with a sponge.

▼ **21.** Place the piece on a dry bat. You can see here that the base is flat and the walls form a right angle.

▼ **22.** The walls are perpendicular to the base, as with a cylinder.

Centerpieces with flat bases and curved walls

Below are instructions on how to make a centerpiece with a flat base like a cylinder and curved walls like a bowl. Most pieces can be done with slight variations on the basic pieces you've studied.

► **1.** Place a large bat on the wheel, center a piece of clay, and flatten it.

▼ **4.** When the center is flat, raise the walls in a curve.

▲ **2.** You can work with your fingertips, pressing downward as you draw the clay toward you.

▲ **3.** You can also draw the clay toward you with the fingertips of your right hand, as you push it in the opposite direction with the palm of your left hand.

▼ **5.** Adjust the thickness.

▼ **6.** Eliminate unnecessary thickness by pressing the clay on the outside of the base.

▲ **7.** Thin the walls, keeping in mind that the base should be a little thicker so that the piece doesn't collapse, since this is a bowl shape.

▲ **8.** Cut the excess clay away from the outer edge of the base with a wooden tool held at an angle. If there's a lot of excess clay, the piece was not thrown properly.

▲ **9.** Then cut the base with the wooden tool held parallel to the wheel so that it cuts a strip of clay.

▲ **10.** Remove the strip, and then cut the base off the bat. To remove it without leaving much clay on the bat, keep the wheel moving and use a cutting wire made from piano wire, keeping it very taut as you cut.

▲ **11.** Allow to dry for a day. When the rim no longer bends, make a chuck. If the mouth of the piece is larger than the wheel, make a conical chuck.

▲ **12.** The rim of the chuck should be fairly thick.

◄ **13.** Use a needle tool to cut off the outer, upper, and inner edges of the rim, to insure that the chuck is completely centered.

▼ **14.** Dry it with a heat gun.

▲ **15.** Place the piece face down on the chuck.

▲ **16.** Center the piece, holding it by the rim, so that it's parallel to the wheel.

▶ **17.** With an angle tool, turn the base parallel to the rim.

▲ **18.** Turn down the diameter of the base.

▲ **19.** Use a wire loop tool to adjust the contours of the piece, making sure to follow the inside shape.

▲ **20.** Finish off the contours with a flexible rib held perpendicular to the wheel.

◀ **21.** If you want to close the pores, you can go over the piece with the flexible rib held parallel to the work.

▶ **22.** With a small trimming tool, mark off the foot ring.

► **23.** Since this is a recessed rather than a raised foot ring, simply hollow out the inside.

▼ **25.** Flatten the base with a rectangular flexible rib.

▲ **24.** A large surface is easier to work with a wire loop tool, as long as the base is not too moist.

◄ **26.** Go over it with a sponge to finish the turning.

◄ **27.** Wash your hands well and remove the piece from the wheel, holding it under the rim. Allow to dry for a day face down on a bat.

► **29.** Cut the inner and outer edges of the rim and use the heat gun to dry only the inside areas that will come into contact with the piece.

► **28.** Make the chuck wider, as it will have to accommodate the piece inside it. Cut the upper edge of the rim.

◄ **30.** Holding the piece by the walls, center it on the chuck.

► **31.** Work on the inner base with a trimming tool.

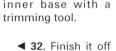

◄ **32.** Finish it off with a flexible rib and go over it with a sponge.

▼ **33.** Remove from the wheel and place on a bat to dry.

▼ The pieces shown below were done by the author using the method described above. The base is even and the walls are fairly thick and curved.

▼ You can also close the mouth of the piece even more; you simply have to use more material.

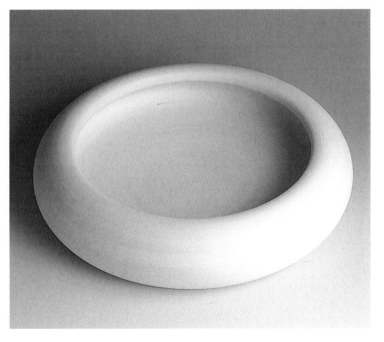

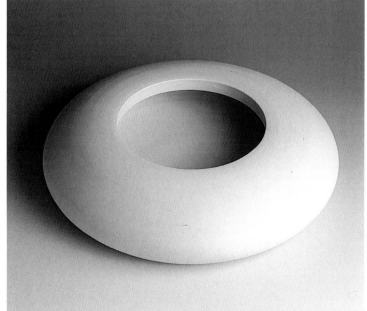

How to make a large piece without centering the clay

Tradition has taught us to center the clay on the wheel before beginning to work. But not all ceramists observe this rule. Now you'll see how to make a piece without centering the clay first.

If you are unsuccessful at first, try again using a softer or harder clay body. Sometimes you don't succeed in making a particular shape because you're using the wrong material.

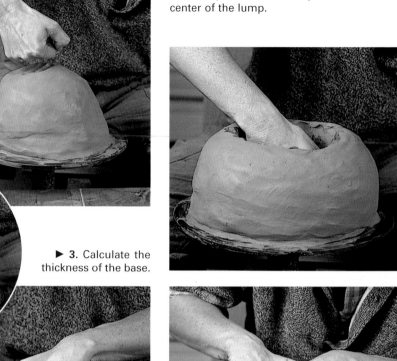

◄ **1.** Place a wide, low lump of clay on the stationary wheel. Insert your fist into the center of the lump.

► **2.** Press down with your fist to open a hole.

► **3.** Calculate the thickness of the base.

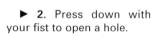

▲ **4.** Start the wheel and wet the outside of the clay as you continue to work.

▲ **5.** Then wet the inside.

▲ **6.** Work on the inside to distribute the clay.

◄ **7.** Remove any lumps of clay that stick to your hands. This can happen depending on the type of clay and the amount of water used.

► **8.** Work on the outside to straighten the walls.

▲ **9.** Next, work on the top part to even out the rim.

▲ **10.** For better control, make the rim go in slightly. It's easier to make this piece if you work a section at a time. First you work on the inside, then the outside, then the upper part. When you've mastered the wheel, you can do these all at once.

▲ **11.** Before pulling the clay up, make sure the walls are uniform.

◀ **13.** Once the clay in the walls is evenly distributed, you can start to shape the piece.

▲ **12.** Pull the clay up.

▶ **14.** You can widen the mouth by pressing on the inside with your left hand.

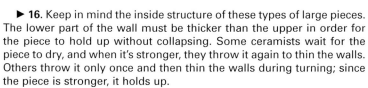

▶ **15.** Give the piece its final shape. If you want the rim to be parallel to the wheel, trim it.

▶ **16.** Keep in mind the inside structure of these types of large pieces. The lower part of the wall must be thicker than the upper in order for the piece to hold up without collapsing. Some ceramists wait for the piece to dry, and when it's stronger, they throw it again to thin the walls. Others throw it only once and then thin the walls during turning; since the piece is stronger, it holds up.

The thickness of the piece depends on the type of clay and how hard it is. The more you practice making a particular piece, the thinner you can make it.

How to make a large piece with less effort

The following method can be used to make a large piece without working all the clay at once—consequently, with less effort. It can also be used if about twenty percent of your plates or centerpieces end up cracking. This means they were not compressed enough at the base. The clay will be more compacted if you compress it with your feet.

► **1.** Put the clay on the floor or on a piece of wood. Make sure the clay doesn't pick up lumps or impurities.

► **2.** Step on it, going around it in a circle.

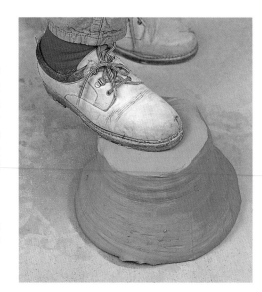

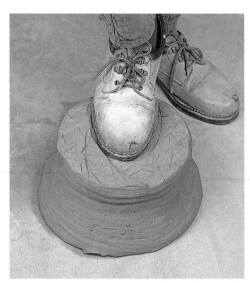

◄ **3.** Continue flattening it . . .

◄ **4.** . . . until you have a large circle of the desired thickness.

▼ **5.** Place a bat on the wheel, and then add the flattened clay. Push the clay toward the center with the palm of your hand, going over the entire surface.

▼ **6.** Repeat the operation in the opposite direction, pushing toward the edges.

▼ **7.** Start the wheel and throw a flat surface, pressing with your fingertips.

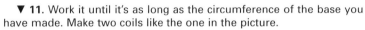
◄ 8. Cut the clay off even with the edge of the bat.

► 9. Next, take another piece of clay and hit it with your hand as you roll it to make it longer.

▼ 10. Roll it with both hands to make it longer and thinner.

▼ 11. Work it until it's as long as the circumference of the base you have made. Make two coils like the one in the picture.

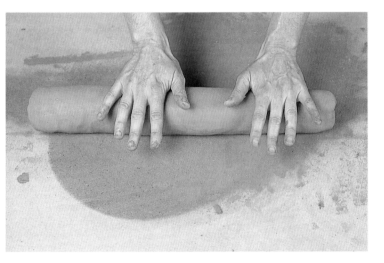

▼ 12. Place the coil along the outer edge of the base.

▼ 13. Next, overlap the two ends and cut them. This way they always meet just right.

▲ **14.** Join the two cut ends. It doesn't matter if one is thicker than the other.

▲ **15.** Press the coil into the base along the outside edge.

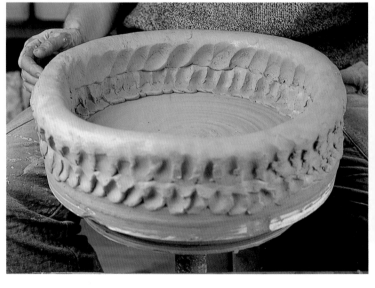

▲ **16.** Then do the same around the base on the inside.

▲ **17.** Then place the second coil on top and repeat the same procedure.

◄ **18.** Begin throwing the piece and center it on the outside.

► **19.** Then throw the inside, making sure the clay is evenly distributed.

► **20.** Raise the walls by pulling the clay up. Finish it off however you wish.

▼ The following pieces were done by the author using the technique just described. Instead of pulling the clay up, it was left in the base to create a thicker piece.

▼ This piece is very solid; it can be made only by applying lots of pressure to the clay.

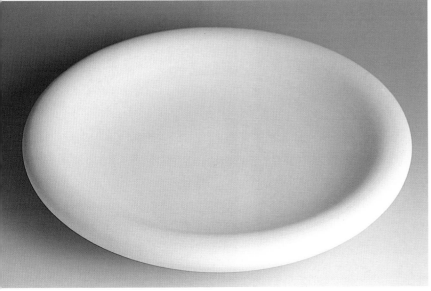

▼ The inside shape of this piece is different from the outside. It's very heavy because it doesn't follow utilitarian guidelines.

▼ Here you can clearly see the difference between the inside and outside shapes. Once you have mastered the basics of throwing, it's a good idea to work freely, using your own ideas and imagination.

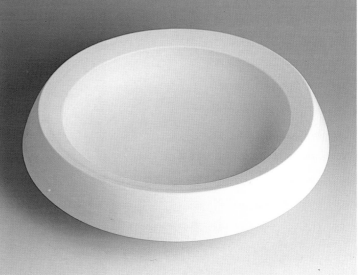

Working like a sculptor

In all the pieces done so far, we have begun with a chunk of clay and shaped it by applying pressure. Now let's make a solid piece and release the shape that's held inside it.

▶ **1.** Throw a flat disc of clay an inch and a half to two inches thick on a plaster bat. Since the bat is made of plaster, use a wooden tool to cut the outside edge.

▶ **2.** Remove rough edges and trim the base of the piece. Allow to dry for three to six days, depending on the room temperature.

▲ **4.** Center the piece, holding it by the rim.

▲ **5.** Flatten both sides of the piece with an angle tool so that it's perfectly uniform.

▲ **3.** When you can scarcely press your thumb into the clay, you can begin turning the piece. Make a flat two-inch-thick chuck on the wheel and dry it with a heat gun a little more than usual, since the chuck will be used for turning a heavy piece.

▶ **6.** Use a wire loop tool to remove material, since the clay is soft.

▶ **7.** As you remove clay, you'll notice that the inside is softer than the outside. Therefore, you can't finish the piece. Shape it with a flexible rib.

► **8.** Turn the disc over and hollow out the inside, since this piece is a small container. Allow it to dry for two more days.

► **9.** Now that the piece is stronger and doesn't lose its shape so easily, center it and cut the outer rim to make sure it's perfectly centered. This operation should be done only if necessary.

► **10.** Even off the rim with a wire loop tool.

▼ **12.** Refine the shape with a flexible rib. Allow it to dry for two more days.

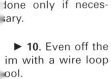

▲ **11.** Round off the edge.

▼ **14.** To remove them, use the same tool held at an angle as shown below, moving it in the opposite direction over the bumps on one side.

► **13.** Turn it again. Note how the tool is held here. Since the clay was soft when you shaped it, the tools left ridges on the surface corresponding to the direction the tool was held.

► **15.** And in the opposite direction to the bumps on the other side.

► **16.** Next, mark out the foot ring and hollow it out.

▼ **17.** Then go over the surface with a sponge and set the piece aside to dry face up.

◄ **18.** Turn the piece over and turn the top. Remove the material with the tool held perpendicular to the piece. Now the tool shouldn't leave any bumps, since the clay is drier.

▼ **19.** Hold the rib at a tight angle to the piece to close up the pores. If you wish, you can burnish the piece.

▼ **20.** Finish turning the center with a small piece of flexible rib.

► **21.** Finally, run the sponge over it.

▼ The pieces shown here were made by the author using the technique just described.

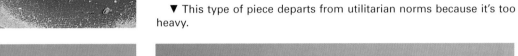

▲ **22.** Then leave it to dry on a dry bat.

▼ This type of piece departs from utilitarian norms because it's too heavy.

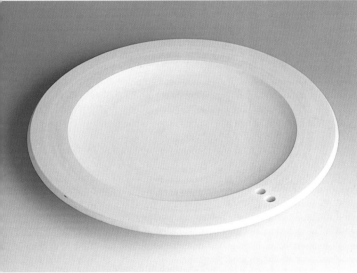

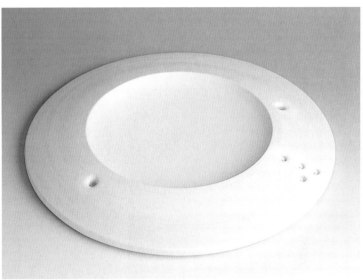

▼ A piece made of refractory clay. You can see the grain on the surface.

▼ This technique is ideal for making thick pieces.

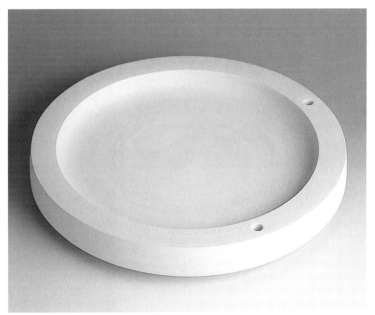

Pots with lids

*P*ots with lids are among the most complex objects. Yet they offer a wide range of creative possibilities in using the wheel. The exercises are explained in simple terms for ease of understanding. But the intent is to show you different ways of making flanges that will allow you to put together some marvelous pieces. Throughout this manual you've been taught to cut the edges of pieces parallel to the wheel head by holding a tool completely level, since this is the best way to ensure that the flanges fit together correctly. You have also learned how to turn pieces so that they fit together precisely.

The main rule to keep in mind is to adjust the two pieces to one another while they both have the same degree of moisture, so that when they're dry they'll fit together as snugly as when they were adjusted. Also, if you fire pots with their lids on, they'll keep their shape.

Let's now begin to examine the various types of flanges required to make these pieces.

Making a foot while turning

The easiest pot to make with a lid is the type in which the foot is made by turning, starting with a fresh lump.

You need to make a flange on only one of the two pieces for them to close properly, although you can choose to make two. Whenever possible, flanges must be made at right angles to fit together correctly.

▲ **1.** It's a good idea to make this piece on a bat so you don't deform the mouth when you remove it from the wheel.

Throw the pot and cut the mouth perfectly parallel to the wheel head and eliminate the rough edges.

▼ **4.** When the two pieces have the same degree of moisture and the mouth of the pot keeps its shape, make the chuck and turn the pot. First flatten the base parallel to the wheel head. This must be done precisely if the two pieces are to fit together properly.

▲ **2.** Use the caliper to measure the outsid[e] diameter at the mouth of the pot and increas[e] the measurement by ³/₄ inch. Cut the piece a[t] the base. If the mouth loses some of its shap[e] when the piece comes loose, don't touch [it] until it has dried a little. That way you'll b[e] able to fix it without damaging it. Another wa[y] to restore roundness to the mouth is to tur[n] the piece while the mouth is still soft enoug[h] to take on the shape of the cone.

▼ **5.** Now turn the walls of the pot.

▲ **3.** Now throw the lid. Place some clay on the bat and flatten it. Scribe the measurement you have taken. Hold the needle tool perpendicular to the base and cut. Let the two pieces dry. Before removing the bat from the wheel, cut the piece off at the base and let the two pieces stand for a day before turning them.

▲ **6**. Adjust the shape with a flexible rib.

▲ **7**. Make the foot ring.

▲ **8**. Now dry your hands well with a towel. With this type of piece, which you are continually handling, you have to keep your hands clean so pieces of clay don't stick to the walls. Dry clay left on your hands after turning easily sticks to the piece when it's removed from the wheel at the end of the process.

▲ **9**. Lift the piece off the wheel and place it onto a bat.

▲ **10**. Now open up the chuck and place the piece upright into it. Use the edge of the wire loop tool to turn the inner surface about a half to three-quarters of an inch from the inside top until it's completely perpendicular to the base, so that the lid will fit properly. Next bevel the inside and outside edges of the mouth.

◄ **12**. Place the lid face down and center it by holding it on the outside. If the lid comes loose while you're turning it, use your fingers to wet the top of step-chuck with a little water.

► **13**. Flatten one side, turn it over, and repeat the procedure on the other side. It's important that the two surfaces be parallel before you make the foot ring.

▲ **11**. Close the chuck up and cut the top part parallel to the wheel head with the needle. If you wish, you can adjust the outside and inside diameters so they're centered correctly.

▲ **14.** Turn the outside of the lid so that it's perpendicular to the base. In other words, the diameter of the top must be the same as the bottom. When you're adjusting the lid, you can remove a little more clay than you did when turning the cylinder. Just add about ⅛ inch more to the original size of the cylinder, or check to be sure that the lid doesn't get smaller.

▲ **15.** Now go over it with the flexible rib to make sure it's even.

▲ **16.** Center the lid again and use the right-angle side of the small trimming tool to cut down the edge. The raised part must be the same size as the mouth of the pot so the two fit together perfectly. Stop cutting before you reach the final dimension, and check before proceeding so you don't accidentally remove too much clay.

▲ **17.** Keep checking it as you turn, until the two parts fit together perfectly. If the piece is big and can't be held in one hand, it should have a knob.

▲ **18.** Next, hollow out the interior as if you were making a foot ring. Throughout this book, we have made perpendicular foot rings so you'd find it easier to make flanges at this point.

▲ **19.** Finally, check the thickness of the piece. The lid should be of uniform thickness so that it shrinks evenly and dries without cracking. Afterwards, go over it with a sponge.

◀ **20.** The piece has been made correctly if the dividing line between the two pieces is parallel to the base and the thickness is the same throughout.

▶ **21.** If you want to alter the shape, turn the upper part of the lid in order to remove the edge and make it more curved. Small variations can produce very different results.

Making a flange while throwing

This type of flange is made in the pot at any desired level while it's being thrown.

If you make the flange 1/4 inch below the rim, the lid can be left solid. If you make it 1/2 inch from the rim, the lid will have to be hollowed out to make it lighter, and so it will sit on the rim of the pot. You can also make the flange thin and place it 1/4–1/2 inch below the rim, in which case it will be recessed. It's important to make a relatively thick flange so it can be turned to form a complete right angle.

In order for the lid to fit perfectly, it's a good idea to make the pot, measure the inside of the mouth, add 1 1/2 inches, and make the lid according to the total measurement. These extra dimensions are needed so you can adjust the two parts correctly and create right angles.

▶ **1.** Place a bat on the wheel and throw a cylinder.
With your left hand supporting the mouth, together with the right index finger, push down toward the wheel head to make the mouth thicker.

▲ **2.** Place your left hand inside the mouth, leaving your thumb outside. Lay the right index finger on its side, exactly in the middle of the rim, and press toward the wheel head. Use the index finger of your left hand to protect the flange from below, while it moves toward the wheel head to the desired area, in this case, about 1/2–3/4 inch from the rim.

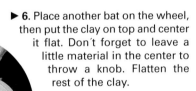

▶ **5.** Use the compass to measure the inside of the mouth where the lid will fit.

▼ **7.** Next, add 1 1/2 inches to the measurement you took of the mouth and mark the new measurement on the lid you have just made.

▲ **3.** Repair the deformation that's occurred on the outside of the piece while making the flange. Cut the mouth parallel to the wheel head and clean up the rough edges left from cutting.

▶ **6.** Place another bat on the wheel, then put the clay on top and center it flat. Don´t forget to leave a little material in the center to throw a knob. Flatten the rest of the clay.

▼ **8.** Check the shape of the knob, cut the lid, and take it off the wheel head. In this case the knob has been thrown very large so different shapes can be tried in the turning process and the right one kept.

▲ **4.** The flange would look like this if it were cut down the middle.

▼ **9.** The knob may break as it's being thrown, or it may turn out too small. If this happens, flatten the center, remove the slip from the middle, dry your hands, and make a ball of clay. Place it in the center and press down on the sides to keep water from getting under it as you throw the knob.

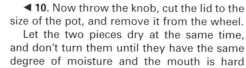

◄ **10.** Now throw the knob, cut the lid to the size of the pot, and remove it from the wheel. Let the two pieces dry at the same time, and don't turn them until they have the same degree of moisture and the mouth is hard enough to keep its shape.

► **11.** When the two pieces have the right amount of moisture, make a cone and place the pot over the chuck. If you're working well and the flange is the right thickness, it won't break. Turn the outside.

▼ **12.** Make the foot ring.

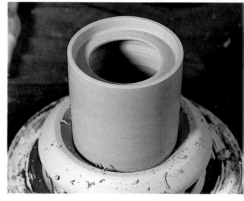

▼ **15.** Close up the chuck and prepare it as if you were about to turn a saucer. The chuck must be smaller in diameter than the lid so you can center the lid easily. The hole needs to be a little bigger than the knob so that it fits inside.

▲ **13.** Open up the chuck as if you were turning a cylinder standing upright, and turn the flange to form a right angle. The flexible rib held vertical or a piece of the same material with a ninety-degree angle is ideal for shaping the flange once it has been turned with a wire loop tool.

▲ **14.** Finally, wipe with a sponge and take it off the wheel.

▼ **16.** Flatten the base of the lid and turn the edge perpendicular to the wheel head. If you turn it convex, the lid will come off easily. Turn the lid over, center it by the outside edge, and turn the knob, trying to keep it completely centered. Once it's centered, it can be adapted to the desired shape. If the lid moves while you're working on it, check the areas where the two pieces rub together. If necessary, modify the chuck or sprinkle a few drops of water onto the top with your fingers to secure it better.

▼ **18.** When the piece is a little drier, as you can see in this pot by its color, thin the knob slightly so it looks more graceful. Next, leave the pot to dry covered, provided the two pieces have been made to fit each other with clay of the same moisture content. If the lid was drier than the pot when you fit it, when the pot dries it will be too small for the lid and may break. If the lid was more moist than the pot, once it's dry it won't fit the way it did when you made it; but you can leave it to dry covered, since that won't damage the piece.

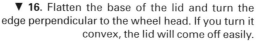

◄ **17.** The exact size is obtained by checking it from time to time while you're turning it. Failure to do this will result in removing too much clay, and the lid won't fit. It's a good idea to throw two lids for each pot just in case something goes wrong.

Another type of flange

This flange is also made at the time of throwing, and it offers numerous possibilities.

Some shapes can serve the purpose of a flange, as you will see in the present exercise. Depending on the size and design of the lid, you can create a wide range of pieces.

▶ **1.** Center the clay and throw a cylinder with thick walls. You can also throw it thin and leave it thicker where the flange will be.

▲ **2.** Close in the mouth of the piece. With the fingers of your left hand placed on the rim of the piece, except for the thumb, grasp the neck and draw it toward the center, while your right index finger controls the edge.

◀ **4.** Cut the flange with a needle tool to center it completely.

▲ **3.** Use your right hand to press the clay between the knuckles of your index and middle fingers to raise the flange, while your left hand supports the piece and your thumbs work together.

▶ **5.** Cut the rim and clean up the rough edges in the area of the cut.

▲ **6.** Now verify the thickness of the cut edges, and check the shape.

▶ Various procedures can produce the same results on the outside.

▶ The pot on the left is the one that was thrown; its lid is a small cylinder. They were turned on cone-shaped chucks. The one on the right is easier to throw but more complicated to turn. The flange was made when the piece was turned, using a small trimming tool.

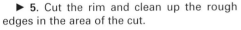

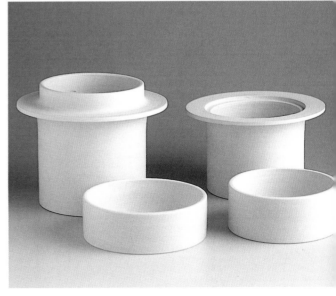

Pots with two-piece lids

This type of pot with a lid is one of the traditional ones that were used in pharmacies for storing products. This container is made in four stages and should be thrown on a bat. Otherwise, it will lose its shape when you remove it from the wheel.

▶ **1.** Throw a cylinder on a bat and draw the neck in.

▶ **2.** Shape the piece as if you were making a rounded vase and collar it some more.

▲ **3.** Throw the neck perfectly straight, even out the walls, and cut the rim parallel to the base.

▲ **4.** Smooth off the rough edges left from the cut.

▲ **5.** Next measure the inside diameter of the neck and add about ⅛ inch.

◀ **7.** If you were to cut the flange, it should have the thickness shown in the photograph so it can be refined by turning. It's a good idea to throw more than one lid.

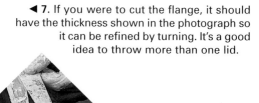

◀ **6.** Throw the lid. In this case it's similar to a bowl. To make the flange, keep some extra clay in the rim of the piece. Press toward the wheel with your right thumb in the center of the rim, keeping your index finger underneath to protect the outer flange. Control the flange with your left index finger on the top and your left middle finger on the inside, creating a flange at a right angle.

◀ **8.** Adjust the outer edge of the flange to the measurement previously taken, plus ⅛ inch. Cut the base of the lid and allow to dry until both pieces have the same degree of moisture and the pot no longer bends at the rim. This lid is curved inside rather than flat, so that when turning, the inside contour follows the outside.

▲ 9. The next day, when both pieces have attained the same hardness, make a chuck and place the piece face down on it.

▶ 11. Use a needle tool to score the area on the base where the foot will be located. Make some concentric circles and then some wavy ones.

◀ 10. Level the base so that it's parallel to the rim and reduce its circumference. Don't turn anything else on the piece, as the material removed could be needed when adjusting the two pieces to fit each other.

◀ 12. Add some slip to the scored area.

◀ 13. Measure the outside diameter of the scored area.

▼ 14. Center some clay on another wheel and open it up.

▼ 15. Throw a cylinder with a hole that reaches all the way to the wheel.

▼ 16. Make the mouth thicker by pressing down toward the wheel. If the walls were pulled up off center, it's best to cut them before making the rim thicker to create the foot.

▲ **17.** Cut the piece at the base with a needle tool.

▶ **18.** Turn the piece over and place the thicker side on the scored area. This must not be too hard, or the two parts won't join properly. If the slip is too shiny, the pieces will slide when you put them together. Press along the inside and the outside with the tips of your index fingers.

▲ **20.** Remove the piece from the wheel and cover it, leaving exposed the part you've just thrown.

▲ **19.** Throw the foot carefully, first downward to avoid disturbing the joint, and then upward to create the desired shape.

◀ **21.** Place the lid on the chuck and adjust the shape where the knob will be. Don't turn the lid any more.

▼ **23.** Score the center using a needle tool, just as you did with the other piece.

▶ **22.** With a flexible rib, refine the contours.

▲ **24.** Apply some slip and allow to dry until it no longer shines.

▲ **25.** Make a ball, place it on the center, and apply pressure around the base with your finger to make sure no water gets in when you throw.

▲ **26.** Then throw the knob. If you haven't learned to throw without water, you won't be able to make this piece. As you can see in the photo, some water has fallen onto the lid. If it had gotten any wetter, the whole piece would have been ruined.

▲ **27.** Consider the shape you want to end up with, and finish it up.

▲ **28.** Remove the lid from the wheel, place it on a clean bat, and cover the hardest area with plastic. Turn the two pieces only when they have reached the same degree of hardness.

▶ **29.** If both pieces have not been thrown correctly, they won't fit one another, as in the photo. For the pieces to fit correctly you have to turn the flange at a right angle. The inside rim of the pot must also be turned so that it's perfectly straight. A precise fit between these pieces is achieved only by turning.

▼ **30.** First, turn the pot face down, using the same type of chuck as for turning a cylinder. Center it by the rim, making sure the body is centered as well. Thin the walls to make them even.

▲ **31.** Adjust the shape with a flexible rib that's curved on one side and straight on the other.

▲ **32.** Turn the piece over and finish turning the upper part using the same chuck.

▲ **34.** Then turn the lid, first working on the neck with the curved side of a small trimming tool, and then turn the rest of it.

▲ **35.** When you're done, go over it with a sponge.

▲ **33.** Smooth the inner wall so that it's perpendicular to the wheel and the flange fits in properly.

▶ **36.** Modify the chuck so that it's thicker on top. Cut the inside edge at an angle to the wheel.

▶ **37.** Center the lid, holding it by the rim.

▲ **38.** Turn the flange with a loop tool.

▲ **39.** Refine the right angle. It's important to keep checking the size of the flange to make sure it will fit. When it fits, stop turning. If you remove too much clay, it won't fit right.

▲ **40.** Once you're done, go over it with a sponge.

▲ **41.** Place the lid on the pot and analyze the piece.

▲ **42.** If you have made additional lids, you can turn them too.

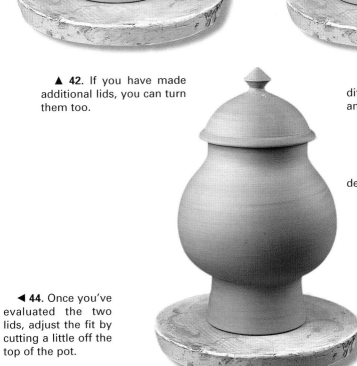

▲ **43.** Turn the second lid differently from the first one and compare the results.

◄ **45.** Finally, choose the desired lid.

◄ **44.** Once you've evaluated the two lids, adjust the fit by cutting a little off the top of the pot.

Two pieces in one

In one type of pot, the flange is made by turning. This type of flange is called a box groove, and it's made in the wall of the piece. Once you have learned to make this joint, you can apply it to various purposes. Do this exercise after you have mastered turning. If you try it before you have learned to center well, or if you turn off center, the pieces won't mate properly and the area of the joint will be uneven.

► **1.** Center the clay on a bat, open it up, and make a cylinder. Neck it and then close it off completely, removing the extra clay.

▲ **2.** Next, use a rib to smooth off the surface and refine the shape.

◄ **3.** Press hard on the top to compress the clay and prevent it from cracking as it dries. Allow to dry for one day and puncture the base to allow the air to escape and keep the piece from cracking.

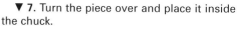

▲ **4.** When the piece is no longer soft and is ready for turning, make a chuck like the one for turning the rim of a cylinder. If you begin turning when the piece is too soft, you may ruin your work.

▲ **5.** Center the piece well and flatten the top.

▼ **7.** Turn the piece over and place it inside the chuck.

▼ **8.** Turn the upper part.

▲ **6.** Next, turn the wall with a rib. If the rib turns properly without skipping, the piece has the right degree of moisture for cutting. Go over the surface with a flexible rib to adjust the lines of the piece.

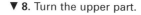

▲ **9.** Then turn the walls as you did on the other side.

▲ **10.** The photo shows the piece after it's been turned.

▲ **11.** Center the piece very precisely. If the top isn't parallel to the wheel, the exercise won't come out correctly. Take a thin utility knife with no rust on the blade; remove any rust with sandpaper. With less than an inch of the blade exposed so it won't bend while you work, cut into the piece parallel to the wheel. You can also do this with a needle tool.

◀ **12.** When you cut into the piece with the blade, it may be helpful to hold the piece by the top. As you cut, it may be better to hold the piece on the side with your left hand, moving to the top when the piece is cut almost through so it doesn't fall off when it comes loose.

▼ **14.** Bevel the inner and outer edges with a wire loop tool to remove the sharp edges left after the cut.

▶ **13.** Center the remaining piece again inside the chuck.

◀ **15.** With the right-angle side of the small loop tool, make a groove in the middle of the rim, then work it downward to create a step. Make sure you have a good grip on the tool with your right hand while resting it on your left thumb to keep the tool from slipping. This is a very precise operation.

▶ **16.** Go over the rim with a flexible rib to perfect the right angle so that the lid will fit exactly; otherwise the two pieces won't match.

▲ **17.** Once the step is made, check that it's the same width all the way around, evening it out where necessary. The needle tool works well for this. Remove any rough edges remaining after the cut, blow on the piece to remove any clay shavings from turning, and go over the piece with a sponge.

▲ **18.** Place the other half on the wheel and remove the rough edges remaining after cutting.

▲ **19.** Make sure the rim has the same thickness all the way around, adjusting it if necessary. You can do this with a needle tool or a small trimming tool.

▲ **21.** If you prefer, you can do the entire operation with a piece of flexible rib, although it may sometimes skip and leave bumps, depending on the hardness of the clay.

▲ **22.** Flatten the inside if necessary. If you want, you can turn the walls some as well. In this case, the marks from throwing were left on the walls.

▲ **20.** Make a groove in the center of the rim, and then relieve the edge, but this time on the outside. For the joint to work you have to make half on the outside and half on the inside.

▶ **23.** Repeat the operation with the other part.

▶ **24.** Once the piece is finished, the rims should interlock, one with a lip on the outside, and the other on the inside.

▲ **25.** Make the chuck narrower and place one of the pieces onto it face down. Go over it with a flexible rib to remove any damage caused by the chuck.

▲ **26.** Go over it with a sponge, and then repeat the process with the other piece.

▲ **27.** If the piece was made properly, the dividing line between the two parts will be straight and of an even width all the way around. If the piece was worked off-center or the joint was made uneven, the pieces won't fit the way they should.

▶ With this shape, you can't make the flange as you did with the cylindrical piece. When you make the flange, the two steps are superimposed and the piece is reduced by about $1/64$ inch to almost $1/2$ inch. In the case of this closed shape, the form would have been lost. That's why it has to be made in a different way.

▶ Follow the procedure described previously until you cut the piece in two. At this point, you add a coil of clay to the inside of the rim and make a flange by throwing. Then adjust the fit in the same way as described before.

▶ This piece was made using the method just described.

▶ When you cut the piece in half and add the flange, make sure you don't change the shape of the rim as you throw; otherwise the two halves won't mate. This is the most difficult exercise shown in this book.

Glossary

a

Angle tool: Flat iron strap about eight inches long and an inch wide, with triangular ends bent at right angles in opposite directions. Potters use it for turning and decorating clay vessels on the wheel.

b

Banding wheel. Small turntable used for shaping pottery pieces.

Basin. Round recipient made of enameled iron, porcelain, earthenware, plastic, etc.

Bat. Stand or support for working clay on a wheel or for holding finished pieces as they dry.

Box groove. Groove in the edge of a board that allows dovetailing with another board.

Burnish. To polish by rubbing with a tool to compact and smooth the surface.

c

Caliper. A metal or wooden measuring instrument with adjustable arms, used to gauge thickness or diameter.

Chamois. Piece of leather used by potters to smooth pieces.

Chuck. Clay mold used to support a pot on the wheel head while it is being turned. A mold used in making or shaping a piece.

Clay. Material consisting of aluminum silicate and impurities, and which comes from the earth. When mixed with water, clay forms a very plastic material and hardens when it is fired. It is used to make ceramics.

Compass. Instrument consisting of two pointed legs joined at the top by a pivot so that they can be opened or closed. It is used to draw curves and measure distances.

e

Earth. Combination of mineral and organic particles that comprise soil.

f

Flange. A rim for support, stability, or decoration.

g

Glaze. Vitreous coating that by means of fusion adheres to porcelain, earthenware, metals, and other goods.

Grog. Fired and ground clay whose granules vary in size, with a texture ranging from granulated sugar to flour, and which is added to clay to facilitate the drying process, provide texture, and reduce shrinkage.

h

Hoop tool. Thin metal band bent in a circle, used for removing material in the turning process, similar to a trimming tool.

k

Kiln. Closed space within which, by means of combustion, pieces are fired at high temperatures.

m

Mud. Mixture of dirt and water, especially resulting from rain that accumulates on soil.

n

Needle tool. Steel tool that ends in a point.

p

Pack. To place pottery into a kiln for firing.

Porcelain. Type of fine, transparent, clear, and lustrous earthenware, invented in China and imitated in Europe.

Potter. Person who makes pottery from kiln-fired clay.

Potter's studio. Place where pots of fired clay are made.

Potter's wheel. Machine used for making and turning pottery.

Pottery. Art of making clay ware. Place where it is made. Art and activity of a potter.

Pug mill. Machine for wedging clay before working with it.

r

Rabbet. Groove or thinning of the edge of a board by means of a radiused cut.

Refractory. A clay body that resists the effects of fire without altering its state or disintegrating.

Reservoir. Open reservoirs are used in preparing clay for making ceramics.

Rib. Tool used by potters, consisting of a rectangular piece of steel about three to six inches square. It has a hole in the center through which a finger can be inserted.

It is used to turn the surface of pieces being worked on the wheel.

Rough edges. Surplus material on the edges or the surface of any object.

s

Shino. A type of glaze.

Sieve. Instrument made up of a hoop and a mesh, closed at the bottom. It is used for separating particles of different sizes, such as with flour, whey, etc.

Slip. Water and clay mixture that forms in containers where ceramists wash their hands, on the sponge, and where they toss excess clay removed from soft pieces being worked on the wheel. This thick soup is used for attaching handles and has other uses.

Sponge. Any object that, due to its elasticity, porosity, and softness, can be used as a cleaning utensil.

Stoneware. Combination of fine clay and quartzose sand which, when fired at temperatures between 2200 and 2375° F, starts to vitrify. It is used to make objects that are resistant to fire and acid, and for artistic ceramics.

t

Thread. Long, thin strand made by twisting flax, wool, hemp, or other textile material.

Threshing floor. Area of clear, firm ground, sometimes lined with stones, where grain is threshed.

Throw. To use a potter's wheel to fashion or to round an object.

Tool. An instrument, usually made of iron or steel, used by artisans in their work.

Trimming tool. Wooden handle with a loop of strap iron fixed to one end; used for removing material in the turning process.

Turn. To smooth and perfect the surface of a piece to embellish it and apply the final touches.

v

Vein. A streak or marking of a material whose color, quality, etc., distinguishes it from the mass in which it occurs.

w

Wedge. To prepare clay for working by kneading it with the hands.

Wire loop tool. Wooden handle fitted with wire loops at each end, used in turning pottery pieces on a wheel.

Bibliography
and acknowledgments

Billington, Dora. *The Technique of Pottery*.
New York: Hearthside, 1962.

Bliss, Gill. *Practical Solutions for Potters: Your Top 465 Questions with Thousands of Practical Solutions*. New York: Sterling, 1998.

Chavarria, Joqaquim. *The Big Book of Ceramics: A Guide to the History, Materials, Equipment, and Techniques of Hand-building, Throwing, Molding, Kiln-firing, and Glazing Pottery and other Ceramic Objects*.
New York: Watson-Guptill, 1994.

Christy, Geraldine. *Step-by-Step Art School: Ceramics*. New York: Book Sales, Inc., 1991.

Clark, Kenneth. *The Potter's Manual*.
New York: Book Sales, Inc., 1990.

Curtis, Edmund de Forest. *Pottery: Its Craftsmanship and its Appreciation*.
New York: Harper, 1940.

Dougherty, John W. *Pottery Made Easy*.
New York: Bruce, 1939.

Duke, Harvey. *Pottery and Porcelain*.
New York: Ballantine, 1999.

Halper, Vick. *Clay Revisions: Plate, Cup, Vase*.
Seattle: Seattle Art, 1987.

Morgan, Judith. *An Art Text-workbook: Ceramics*.
Athens, Ohio: University Classics, 1990.

Nelson, Glenn C. *Ceramics: A Potter's Handbook*.
Fort Worth, Texas: HB College Publishers, 1984.

Nigrosh, Leon. *Claywork*.
Worcester, Massachusetts: Davis, 1986.

Obstler, Mimi. *Out of the Earth, Into the Fire: A Course in Ceramic Materials for the Studio Potter*. Westerville, Ohio: American Ceramics, 1996.

Pucci, Cora. *Pottery: A Basic Manual*.
Boston: Little, Brown, 1974.

Rhodes, Daniel. *Clay and Glazes for the Potter*.
Philadelphia: Chilton, 1966.

———. *Stoneware and Porcelain*.
Philadelphia: Chilton, 1968.

Richardson-Hyde, Dawan. *Simple Ceramics*.
Cincinnati, Ohio: Seven Hills, 1996.

Sapiro, Maurice. *Clay: The Potter's Wheel*.
Worcester, Massachusetts: Davis, 1977.

Swant, Dale. *Beginning Ceramics*.
Livonia, Michigan: Scott Publications, 1994.

Wallner, Linda. *Introduction to Pottery*.
New York: Book Sales, Inc. 1995.

Watson, Oliver. *Studio Pottery*.
San Francisco: Chronicle Books, 1993.

Wensley, Doug. *Pottery: A Manual of Techniques*.
No. Pomfret, Vermont: Crowood Press, 1992.

Winkley, David. *Pottery*.
Orlando, Florida: Drake Publishing, 1974.

I wish to express my gratitude to the Massana School in Barcelona where I have participated in pottery classes for so many years.

Also to my students for their contribution, since without them I wouldn't have experience in the field of teaching.

To Beli Riera, who was always willing to answer any queries I had, especially in the chapter on the history of the potter´s wheel and the glossary, and for making it all fall into place.

To J.V. for his patience, advice, and corrections.

To the potters Salomó and Cornellá, to the Ceramics School, and the Terracotta Museum at La Bisbal.

To the Arcillas Coladas, Inc. factory.

To the ceramists of Esparreguera Feliu Trujillo and Jaume Bosch.

To Mª Fernanda Canal, for the confidence placed in me throughout this project, and to all those who made this book possible.

And finally, I am extremely grateful once again to everyone who helped me with my previous book Secrets of the Potter's Wheel, *since part of this work is based on my experiences with my earlier publication.*